Asmina

CW00348015

CONTENTS

UNIT

1

Pinecones

Autumn 1943. I was four and a half and my brother was three. We'd moved out of Bradford two years earlier to escape the bombing. We lived in a country cottage with gaslight and no running water. There were just the two of us and Mum. Dad was away fighting the Germans. I couldn't remember a time when he wasn't, so I thought that was what dads did – fight the Germans.

I'd no idea what Germans were. I'd got the word German and the word germ mixed up in my mind. There was a disinfectant ad in the papers which showed germs as little black bugs with lots of legs. There was another ad too, about not wasting food. It had a creature called the squanderbug in it. The squanderbug had big, sharp teeth and a fat, hairy body with swastikas all over it. I thought Germans were something like that.

On Thursdays my mum had to take my brother to the clinic in the nearest town. It was two miles. There were no buses. I walked, and Mum pushed Donald in his pushchair.

One Thursday morning we set off as usual. It had been a windy night, and fallen leaves lay in drifts along the lane. It was my first all-walking autumn, and I started kicking showers of leaves in the air as we went along. Mum was a fast walker, and I kept having to run to catch up.

We rounded a bend. The fallen leaves thinned and ceased. The trees which overhung this stretch were dark pines. They tossed in the gusty wind. As we walked under them I saw strange objects scattered on the wet tarmac.

I stopped, squatting to examine one. Mum strode on. I touched the thing with my mitten. It rolled. I picked it up, knowing I shouldn't. There was a rumour that the Germans were dropping small, brightly-coloured bombs for children to find, and I wasn't supposed to pick things up. Nothing dreadful happened, so I straightened up and ran after Mum with the thing in my hand.

"What's this, Mummy?" I said, opening my mitten.

"That's a pinecone," she told me. She pointed to the trees.

"Those are pine trees. Pinecones grow on them. They have seeds inside to make new pine trees."

"Can I keep it?" I asked.

She laughed. "Yes. Gather some more, and we'll take them home. They make a lovely blaze when you put them on the fire." I thought they were far too nice to put on the fire, but I scampered about picking up cones till my pockets bulged and Mum was way out in front.

Presently there was a noise like a motorbike coming down the lane, and I did as I had been taught, trotting to the verge and standing still. Mum turned the pushchair and began running back towards me. I'd never seen Mum run before. She looked frightened, and that scared me. She grabbed me, dumped me on top of Donald and crouched over us as the engine noise grew to a roar you could feel through the soles of your feet. After a moment the noise receded and she stood up, lifting me off the pushchair. "What was it?" I asked.

"A German aeroplane," said Mum.

I had to hold onto the pushchair the rest of the way. We passed some good pinecones, but we didn't stop.

The next day, rolling pinecones about on the stone floor of our big kitchen, I listened as Mum and Mrs Applegate from next door talked about the aeroplane. It had come down somewhere nearby, and the four Germans inside had been given tea at a farmhouse before the police came to take them away.

As I listened, it dawned on me that Germans were just people. This filled me first with amazement, then with disappointment. No fangs, then. No black hair or extra legs. Just people who sat in kitchens like Mum and Mrs Applegate, drinking tea.

Pinecones were far more interesting.

Robert Swindells from *Autobiography, ed. John Foster* (Oxford University Press)

1   Explain what is meant by "first all-walking autumn" in paragraph four. *(1 mark)*

2   List four different facts that we are told about the country cottage where
    the Swindells lived. *(2 marks)*

3   Why had Mrs Swindells and her two sons moved to the cottage in 1941? *(1 mark)*

4   Which word in paragraph six indicates, as Robert Swindells says, that Mum
    was "a fast walker"? *(1 mark)*

5   How might the picture of the squanderbug have helped to stop people from
    wasting food during the Second World War? Give all the good reasons you
    can think of. *(3 marks)*

6   Why did Robert hesitate before picking up the pinecone in paragraph six? *(1 mark)*
    a) It was covered in germs.
    b) It might have been a bomb.
    c) Pinecones catch fire easily.
    d) He might have been left behind.

7   Why did Robert have to hold on to the pushchair for the rest of the journey?
    (1 mark)
    a) He had collected too many pinecones.
    **b) They were going to be late for Donald's appointment at the clinic if they weren't
    careful.**
    c) His mother was anxious about their safety and didn't want to linger.
    d) He was in disgrace.

8   What evidence is there in the passage to suggest that Robert was usually an
    obedient child? *(2 marks)*

9   Which word from the list below best describes Robert's mother? Explain your
    choice by referring to an incident in the passage as evidence. (Use a dictionary
    to check meanings if you wish.) *(1 mark)*
    a) houseproud
    b) protective
    c) negligent
    d) lazy
    e) flippant

10 Give two reasons why "Pinecones" is a good title for this true-life account. *(2 marks)*

The granny project

The doctor was having a hard time with the Harris family. He'd been around to their house often enough before, of course. He'd been their family doctor for years. He'd seen them bellowing red-faced in cots, or miserably picking at their chicken poxes, or coughing horribly in steamed-up bathrooms. He'd never seen them all together in one room, and well, before. The noise was appalling. The four of them, two girls, two boys, sat round the kitchen table eating like wolves. There was much scraping of knives and grating of forks. All the plates rattled on the table top. They were, the doctor realised after a moment's perplexed reflection, all seconds, warped in the kiln and sold off cheaply in the market. The children didn't seem to notice the clatter, or that their plates were wobbling horribly. They sat, hunched over, eating very fast. The elder boy's last sausage, stabbed too hard, spun off the plate on to the floor where he immediately swooped to stab it with his fork again.

"No need to kill your food. It is already dead."

The beautiful Natasha Dolgorova spoke from where she leaned, distant and contemptuous, against the airing cupboard door.

The doctor sighed. You'd never think she was their mother, he thought. She acted as if they were nothing at all to do with her, some horrible mistake, just for today, this houseful of children; as if the next-door roof had blown off in the night and she, a cool exotic childless woman, was just for once forced into looking after them.

"Nor is it poisoned. And so you need not spit it on the plate."

"That's gristle, that is!"

"Tssssk!"

She hissed so fiercely, the doctor jumped. None of the children took the slightest notice. The doctor hurriedly went on with filling in the form in front of him.

"Osteoarthritis," he muttered, scribbling in yet another large blank. "Metacarpophalangeal joint involvement leading to characteristic volar subluxation and ulner deviation of the phalanges..."

"What?"

Henry Harris, the children's father, sunk in gloom beside the vegetable rack, was suddenly deeply suspicious.

"He says your old mother's fingers are bent."

"Ah." ⇨

5

"Degenerative changes in the cochlea ..."

"And she goes deaf."

"Right."

"Impairment of brain tissue function with concomitant deterioration of cognitive functioning ..."

"And stupid, too."

"Natasha!"

"Tssssk!"

The doctor kept his head well down.

"She's still smart enough to get to the newspaper every morning before anyone else," Sophie said.

"What's in a newspaper to interest you?" Natasha demanded of her elder daughter.

"Stuff. Stuff for projects. Any old stuff."

Her brother, Ivan, laughed through his mouthful of chips.

"Everything interests me and Sophie," he said. "Now we do Social Science. Crime, Violence, Police Corruption and Consumer Protection, Race Relations, Suicide Rates, Sex Statistics –"

"Tsssk!" Natasha Dolgorova hissed at her son who, grinning, tossed his dark curls back at her and calmly went on sopping up leftover ketchup with his bread.

"Projects! Pah! Such a school! I'll take you out of it! *Projects!*"

"There's no specific ambulatory problems, I take it."

"The lazy old woman can still walk, yes. If she is truly hungry."

The doctor winced.

"More of a shuffle, really," Sophie said.

"Well, that's because she stole my bedroom slippers," Henry Harris explained to the doctor mournfully. "They're several sizes too large for her feet."

"Her dietary intake?"

"The woman can eat *anything*."

The depth of Natasha's scorn was unmistakable.

"It's true," Henry Harris had to admit.

"She ate the leaves off Sophie's geranium last week," Ivan said, trouble-making. "And Nicholas and Tanya caught her chewing feathers this morning."

"You did?" Natasha asked the younger pair.

"A few," said Nicholas, playing it down.

"Lots," Tanya declared, exaggerating.

"See! Stupid and greedy, that is what she is!"

"Natasha! Please!"

"And she should know the *cost* of pillows."

"Ssssh."

"*Tsssssk*, yourself, Henry Harris! She is not *my* mother!"

The doctor, folding back another side of paper, suddenly spotted the end of the form. He cheered enough to say:

"One further manifestation, should we seek it, of the proven versatility of the human gastro-intestinal tract."

"Just what I said," Natasha Dolgorova claimed. "The woman can eat anything."

The doctor rose. He tapped the forms.

"I'll see that these get to the right place," he said. "But since there's no immediate problem – " Catching one of Natasha's venomous looks he hastily amended this to – "since Mrs Harris isn't actually *ill* at present, results may not be immediate, you understand. But I'll do what I can."

The children all stopped clattering to lift their heads and look at him. Then Ivan said:

"What does he mean? Results? What's going on? Are you two thinking of putting Granny into a Home?"

"Thinking is finished," Natasha told him. "It is decided."

"Dad?"

Henry Harris blushed.

"*Dad?*"

"Your mother and I are finding Granny an enormous strain," he began.

"You're never sending Granny *away*?"

"Nothing's *decided*," Henry Harris said uncomfortably. ▷

"Nothing for you to worry about. Let's wait and see."

Natasha hurled the dirty dishes into the sink.

"Шипа в мешке не утаишь," she said darkly.

"What? What did she say? Dad, what did she just say? What was that?"

The panic was traditional. Natasha's proverbs were notorious.

Sometimes it appeared to Henry that the only thing his wife had brought with her when she defected to the West was a seemingly inexhaustible supply of ominous sayings.

"What did that mean, Dad?"

"Nothing."

"Dad!"

Henry Harris dropped his head in shame, and translated:

"You can't hide sharp steel spikes in soft cloth bags."

The children held their meeting at the back of the garage. Sophie let Ivan take the comfy tyre and sat down on the upturned tea-chest. Tanya and Nicholas perched on the bonnet of the car.

"First thing," said Ivan. "Do we care?"

Four hands went up.

"Next thing," said Ivan. "Do we believe that we can stop them?"

Four hands went up again.

"Last thing," said Ivan. "How?"

The pause that followed did not last for long. Tanya suggested frequent bouts of tears, and screaming nightmares featuring Granny chained to an iron bedstead in the Home, starving and lonely, missing them all. Ivan put forward the idea of a strike: not fetching in the coal, no washing-up, refusals to run down to the shops. Nicholas thought that the strike should go further, that they should all refuse to speak, except to one another or Granny, until the whole idea was dropped for good. Sophie was silent, still thinking hard, till all of their ideas ran out and they turned round to look at her.

"Well?" Ivan said. "Sophie?"

"Listen," said Sophie. "This project that was set last week –"

"For Social Science?"

"Yes."

"Well?"

"You and me, Ivan, we'll team up for it. We'll work together, doing a joint project, double the length."

"On?"

"Ageing people in the community."

Ivan grinned. Tanya and Nicholas looked blank. Sophie went on: "We'll get the statistics stuff from newspapers and reference books. That won't take long. But half the project, a good half of it, will be a fairly vivid and uncensored description –"

Ivan broke in:

"Of one particular family!"

Anne Fine from *The Granny Project* (Methuen)

Answer in sentences.

1 In what ways was the doctor "having a hard time" with the Harris family? *(1.5 marks)*

2 Why did the doctor visit the Harris family if no one was ill? Was it a social visit? *(2 marks)*

3 Explain in your own words what was making the plates wobble so much. *(1 mark)*

4 Why was the doctor keeping "his head well down"? *(1 mark)*

5 What made the doctor feel that Natasha Dolgorova was behaving like "a cool exotic childless woman"? *(1.5 marks)*

6 We are told that Natasha Dolgorova was a Russian who had "defected to the West". What does this mean? *(1 mark)*

7 In what ways are Natasha's proverbs correctly described as "ominous", judging from the example here? *(1 mark)*

8 Why did Sophie find newspapers useful for her Social Science projects? *(1 mark)*

9 What is the relevance here of the Russian proverb, "You can't hide sharp steel spikes in soft cloth bags"? *(2 marks)*

10 Find two words (not used together) that show Henry Harris was embarrassed at having to admit to his children that he was planning to move their grandmother into a residential home. *(1 mark)*

11 What made Natasha shoot the doctor "a venomous look" at one point? *(1 mark)*

12 Do you find any evidence in the passage that the grandmother was behaving strangely? Explain. *(1 mark)*

UNIT 3

Battery power

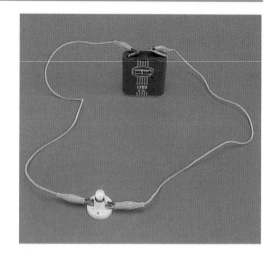

Even though you must never do experiments with mains electricity, you can discover a lot about electricity in complete safety using small batteries and bulbs. Batteries are useful because they are small enough to be carried from place to place.

The first battery

The first battery was made in 1800 by an Italian scientist, Alessandro Volta. Volta discovered that some metals and a liquid could work together to produce electricity.

He made a "sandwich" of paper soaked in salt water between a piece of silver and a piece of zinc. When he joined the two metals with a wire, he found that a current flowed through the wire. As the current was very weak, he made a pile of his "sandwiches" and when he touched a wire from the top of the pile to a wire from the bottom, he got sparks of electricity. Volta's battery came to be known as the **Voltaic pile.**

Did you know that the electrical measurement the **"volt"** was named after Volta? The number of volts describes the pressure or **"voltage"** which pushes electricity along a wire.

How a battery works

The batteries we use today work in a similar way to the battery made by Volta. The case of a battery is made of zinc metal; this is often covered with card and plastic or tin to prevent the battery from leaking. Instead of a piece of silver or copper, there is a carbon rod (rather like a thick pencil lead) in the middle of the battery. The battery case is not filled with salt water because this would easily leak out. Instead, there is a chemical paste between the carbon and the zinc casing.

The chemicals in the battery make electricity. As the electricity is taken from the battery, the chemicals are slowly used up. Eventually, the battery cannot make electricity any more. Some batteries, such as those used in cars, can be recharged so they go on working for longer.

Make your own battery

Equipment:

Two pieces of wire about 30 cm long, sticky tape,
4 copper coins, 4 pieces of zinc, blotting paper soaked in salty water.

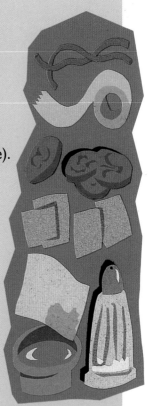

1. Sandwich a piece of the salty blotting paper between a coin and a piece of zinc (ask an adult to cut this for you from a battery case).
2. Tape the bare end of one wire to the coin.
3. Now make three more sandwiches and add them to the first.
4. Finally, tape the bare end of the other wire to the piece of zinc on the bottom of your Voltaic pile.
5. Now take the free end of each wire and touch both ends lightly on to your tongue. Can you feel a tingle of electricity?

How it works

In your Voltaic pile, chemical reactions cause a tiny electric current. The current flows from one wire through your tongue and into the other wire. The current is just enough to make your tongue tingle.

Can you get electricity from a lemon?

Make two slits in the skin of a lemon and push a copper coin into one slit and a piece of zinc into the other slit. Make sure the two metals are not touching each other inside the lemon. If you hold the coin and the zinc gently against your tongue, you should be able to feel a tingle of electricity.

The current flows because a chemical reaction takes place between the metals and an acid in the lemon juice. The lemon juice acts in the same way as Volta's salt water or the chemical paste in the battery.

Terry Cash and Steve Parker from *More Fun With Science*
(Kingfisher Books)

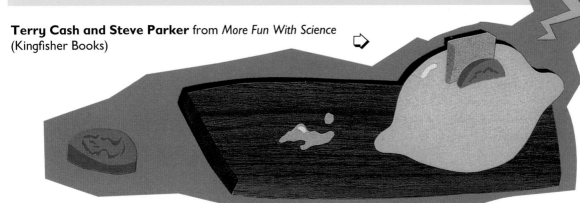

11

1   What is used in batteries today instead of salt water? *(1 mark)*

2   Why did Volta need to put lots of "sandwiches" together when he made the first battery? *(1 mark)*

3   Write out the statements that are true: *(3 marks)*

   a) The inventor of the first battery was an Italian scientist.
   b) There is a small current of electricity in a ripe lemon.
   c) Alessandro Volta made the first ever battery in 1880.
   d) You need two different metals in a Voltaic pile.
   e) Your tongue completes the circuit in the lemon experiment.

4   If you make your own Voltaic pile (according to the instructions "Make your own battery"), which metal will end up at the bottom of the pile, and which at the top? *(1 mark)*

5   In the lemon experiment, why do you have to make sure that the two metals are not touching inside the lemon? *(1 mark)*

6   What is used instead of silver or copper in a modern battery? *(1 mark)*

7   Explain why batteries "run out". *(2 marks)*

8   Why is salt water not used in modern batteries? *(1 mark)*

   a) It would be against the conservation laws.
   b) It wouldn't work in modern batteries.
   c) It would easily leak out.

9   Why is it highly dangerous to experiment with mains electricity or large batteries? *(2 marks)*

10 Which electrical term has been named after Alessandro Volta and what does it mean? *(2 marks)*

A note about the next story

Roald Dahl adds this author's note in one collection of his short stories to explain how he came to write "The Mildenhall Treasure".

In 1946, more than thirty years ago, I was still unmarried and living with my mother. I was making a fair income by writing two short stories a year. Each of them took four months to complete, and fortunately there were people both at home and abroad who were willing to buy them.

One morning in April of that year, I read in the newspaper about a remarkable find of Roman silver. It had been discovered four years before by a ploughman near Mildenhall, in the county of Suffolk, but the discovery had for some reason been kept secret until then. The newspaper article said it was the greatest treasure ever found in the British Isles, and it had now been acquired by the British Museum. The name of the ploughman was given as Gordon Butcher.

True stories about the finding of really big treasure send shivers of electricity all the way down my legs to the soles of my feet. The moment I read the story, I leapt up from my chair without finishing my breakfast and shouted goodbye to my mother and rushed out to my car. The car was a nine-year-old Wolseley, and I called it "The Hard Black Slinker". It went well but not very fast.

Mildenhall was about a hundred and twenty miles from my home, a tricky cross-country trip along twisty roads and country lanes. I got there at lunchtime, and by asking at the local police station, I found the small house where Gordon Butcher lived with his family. He was at home having his lunch when I knocked on his door.

I asked him if he would mind talking to me about how he found the treasure.

"No, thank you," he said. "I've had enough of reporters. I don't want to see another reporter for the rest of my life."

"I'm not a reporter," I told him. "I'm a short-story writer and I sell my work to magazines. They pay good money." I went on to say that if he would tell me exactly how he found the treasure then I would write a truthful story about it. And if I was lucky enough to sell it, I would split the money equally with him. ▷

In the end, he agreed to talk to me. We sat for several hours in his kitchen, and he told me an enthralling story. When he had finished, I paid a visit to the other man in the affair, an older fellow called Ford. Ford wouldn't talk to me and closed the door in my face. But by then I had my story and I set out for home.

The next morning, I went up to the British Museum in London to see the treasure Gordon Butcher had found. It was fabulous. I got the shivers all over again just from looking at it.

I wrote the story as truthfully as I possibly could and sent it off to America. It was bought by a magazine called the *Saturday Evening Post*, and I was well paid. When the money arrived, I sent exactly half of it to Gordon Butcher in Mildenhall.

One week later, I received a letter from Mr Butcher written upon what must have been a page torn from a child's school exercise-book. It said "... you could have knocked me over with a feather when I saw your cheque. It was lovely. I want to thank you ..."

Here is the story almost exactly as it was written thirty years ago. I've changed it very little. I've simply toned down some of the more flowery passages and taken out a number of superfluous adjectives and unnecessary sentences.

Roald Dahl from *The Wonderful Story of Henry Sugar* (Puffin)
"The Mildenhall Treasure" was published in an earlier version in the *Saturday Evening Post*

Answer in sentences.

1   How did Roald Dahl first hear about the discovery of the treasure
    in Mildenhall? *(1 mark)*

2   What actions tell us that he was extremely excited at the news of the discovery?
    (2 marks)

3   Why do you think Gordon Butcher never wanted to see another reporter in
    his life? *(1 mark)*

4   Which words reveal that it took some time to persuade Gordon Butcher to tell
    Roald Dahl his story? *(1 mark)*

5   Why do you think Gordon Butcher changed his mind and confided in
    Roald Dahl? *(2 marks)*

6   What further research did Roald Dahl do? *(1 mark)*

7   Why do you think Roald Dahl sent the story to the editor of an American
    magazine rather than a British one? *(1 mark)*

8   Explain what Gordon Butcher meant when he said, "You could have knocked
    me over with a feather". *(1 mark)*

9   Give the meaning of these words as used in the passage:

    a) fair (first paragraph) *(1 mark)*
    b) remarkable (second paragraph) *(1 mark)*
    c) enthralling (fifth paragraph from end) *(1 mark)*
    d) superfluous (last paragraph) *(1 mark)*

10 When Roald Dahl came to revise the story for publication in book form some
    thirty years later, what kind of changes did he make? *(1 mark)*

UNIT 5

The outing

Right, class six
RIGHT, CLASS SIX
I'm talking

I'm talking
I want complete quiet
and that includes you, David Alexander,
yes, you
no need to turn around, David
there aren't any other David Alexanders
        here, are there?
Louise
it isn't absolutely necessary for your watch
to play us London's Burning just now, is it?

Right
as you know
it was our plan to go out today –
to the Science Museum.
Now I had hoped that it would not be
        necessary

for me to have to tell you –
yes, you as well, Abdul,
you're in class six as well, aren't you?
I saw that, Mark,
I saw it.
Any more and you'll be out.
No trip,
nothing.

I had hoped that it wouldn't be necessary
for me to tell you how to BEHAVE
when we go on a trip.

But –
and this is a big but –
you haven't heard a word I've said, have
      you, Donna?
This is a big but
I HAVE to tell you how to behave, don't I?
Why?

Yes, it IS because you never listen
but there's another reason, isn't there?
Yes, Warren,
because of what happened last time.

Let us remind ourselves of a few things:
The food –
Even as I speak
would you believe it?
I can see that Phanh has opened her can of
      drink
I do not believe it
I really don't.
Do we have lunch at nine-thirty at school?
No,
we have lunch at twelve-fifteen
but, Phanh, you've already begun yours.
If you remember,
last time
Joanna had eaten all her sandwiches
before she even got to school.
Lloyd sat on his orange
and burst it
and Alfred put a chocolate swiss roll in his
pocket
and –
yes –
it melted. ⟳

So, remember, lunch is when?
yes yes yes
of course lunch is at lunch time
but when?
twelve-fifteen
correct.

Perhaps, I thought,
when I got up this morning,
I won't have to tell class six
about what to do when we get to the station
but then I remembered
David's little gang
who decided they wouldn't wait for me to
        tell them
what train to get on
and before we all knew it
David and his little gang
were heading for the seaside on their own.

When we get to the museum –
Of course YOU'RE not listening, are you,
        Lydia?
But then of course you didn't listen last time,
        did you?
And then you wondered why
you sat on Lloyd's orange after Lloyd had
        already sat on it once.

When we get to the museum
do we run about the corridors?
Do we run around screaming?
Do we go sliding on the shiny floors?
No we don't
no we don't
no we don't.

Thank you, Mervyn, that's enough.
I'm very glad you've got jam in your
      sandwiches, Mervyn,
we are all glad that you've got jam in your
      sandwiches, Mervyn,

but what has it got to do with sliding on the
      floor of the Science Museum?
Precisely nothing.
I'm very sorry, Mervyn, but nobody,
nobody at all
wants to know about the jam in your
      sandwiches, Mervyn.

Now,
when you're ready
when you're quiet
we'll all go.
That doesn't mean leaping up in the air,
      Karen,
does it?
Louise, why is your watch now playing
For He's a Jolly Good Fellow?
Yes, I know it could be SHE'S A Jolly Good
      Fellow, Zoe,
but that isn't what we are talking about, is
      it?

Mervyn,
if I hear about your sandwiches
your jam
or the jam IN your sandwiches
if I hear about any of it once more
I shall give them to the ducks. ⤸

Yes, John, what do you want?
I don't know what ducks, John.
Any ducks.

Right
when there is complete quiet
complete quiet
you will find your partners and stand by the
    door.

Oh no, not another chocolate swiss roll,
    Alfred, surely not?

Marcia, you cannot have Charmaine AND
    Donna
as your partner
because that makes three
and three does not mean PARTNER,
    does it?
And perhaps you can put your comb in your
    bag for at least three seconds
just giving us enough time to get to the
    door? Mmm?

Good
right, class six, we're off

Why not leave your watch behind, Louise?

Michael Rosen from *The Hypnotiser*
(Scholastic)

20

 Answer in sentences.

1   What three points about behaviour during the outing is the teacher trying to get across? *(1.5 marks)*

2   Why is the second line of the poem in block capitals? *(1 mark)*

3   How can you tell that the teacher is finding it difficult to control the class? *(2 marks)*

4   How does Michael Rosen succeed in making the speaker here sound just like a certain type of teacher? *(4 marks)*

5   Why does the teacher say to Mervyn "Thank you, Mervyn, that's enough"? Enough of what? *(0.5 mark)*

6   What question did John ask the teacher? *(0.5 mark)*

7   Which adjectives from this list accurately describe the teacher in the poem? *(1 mark)*

witty	authoritative	sarcastic
jolly	relaxed	popular
gentle	harassed	kind

8   Do you think the pupils will behave well on the outing? Give your reasons. *(1 mark)*

9   Do you like the last line of the poem as an ending or do you think it would be better to finish the poem a line earlier? Why? *(1.5 marks)*

10 Did you enjoy reading this poem? Give your reasons as clearly as you can. *(2 marks)*

UNIT

6

Anne Frank's diary: 1942

During the Second World War, Hitler aimed to exterminate the Jewish people. He considered them to be an inferior race and blamed them for all of Germany's problems.

The Franks were a Jewish family who had moved to Holland from Germany in 1933. Hitler invaded Holland seven years later, in the early part of the war.

Anne describes in her diary the restrictions the Dutch Jews had to endure after the invasion. They had to sew large yellow stars on their clothes so that they could be easily identified. They weren't allowed to ride bicycles (Margot in the extract is very brave to risk being caught) or drive cars, or travel by train. They were banned from theatres, cinemas, sports grounds and swimming baths. They had to be indoors by 8pm each evening and were never allowed to visit Christian friends. Many thousands were "called up" for forced labour in Germany.

All too often, these conscripts were sent directly to death camps.

Otto Frank, Anne's father, prepared a hiding-place for his family and four close friends above his office and warehouse so that they could escape just such a call-up. They moved into their "Secret Annexe" two days before Anne's first diary entry below. Anne had been given the diary as a present for her thirteenth birthday, the previous month. You will see that she treated the diary as a friend whom she called Kitty.

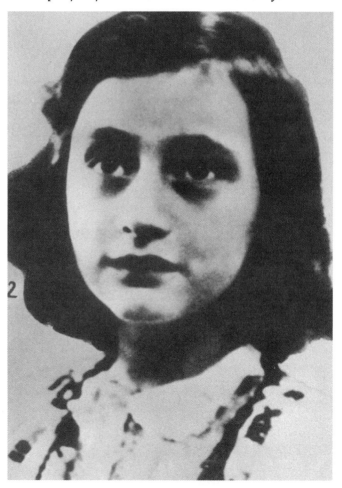

Wednesday, 8th July 1942

Dear Kitty,

Years seemed to have passed between Sunday and now. So much has happened, it is just as if the whole world had turned upside down. But I am still alive, Kitty, and that is the main thing, Daddy says.

Yes, I'm still alive, indeed, but don't ask where or how. You wouldn't understand a word, so I will begin by telling you what happened on Sunday afternoon.

At three o'clock (Harry had just gone, but was coming back later) someone rang the front door bell. I was lying lazily reading a book on the veranda in the sunshine, so didn't hear it. A bit later, Margot appeared at the kitchen door looking very excited. "The S.S. have sent a call-up notice for Daddy," she whispered. "Mummy has gone to see Mr Van Daan already."
(Van Daan is a friend who works with Daddy in the business.) It was a great shock to me, a call-up; everyone knows what that means. I picture concentration camps and lonely cells – should we allow him to be doomed to this? "Of course he won't go," declared Margot, while we waited together. "Mummy has gone to the Van Daans to discuss whether we should move into our hiding-place tomorrow. The Van Daans are going with us, so we shall be seven in all." Silence. We couldn't talk any more, thinking about Daddy, who, little knowing what was going on, was visiting some old people in the Joodse Invalide; waiting for Mummy, the heat and suspense, all made us very overawed and silent.

Suddenly the bell rang again. "That is Harry," I said. "Don't open the door." Margot held me back, but it was not necessary as we heard Mummy and Mr Van Daan downstairs talking to Harry, then they came in and closed the door behind them. Each time the bell went, Margot or I had to creep softly down to see if it was Daddy, not opening the door to anyone else.

Margot and I were sent out of the room. Van Daan wanted to talk to Mummy alone. When we were alone together in our bedroom, Margot told me that the call-up was not for Daddy, but for her. I was more frightened than ever and began to cry. Margot is sixteen; would they really take girls of that age away alone? ⇨

But thank goodness she won't go. Mummy said so herself; that must be what Daddy meant when he talked about us going into hiding.

Into hiding – where would we go, in a town or the country, in a house or a cottage, when, how, where ...?

These were questions I was not allowed to ask, but I couldn't get them out of my mind. Margot and I began to pack some of our most vital belongings into a school satchel. The first thing I put in was this diary, then hair-curlers, handkerchiefs, school books, a comb, old letters; I put in the craziest things with the idea that we were going into hiding. But I'm not sorry, memories mean more to me than dresses.

At five o'clock Daddy finally arrived, and we rang up Mr Koophuis to ask if he could come round in the evening. Van Daan went and fetched Miep. Miep has been in the business with Daddy since 1933 and has become a close friend, likewise her brand-new husband, Henk. Miep came and took some shoes, dresses, coats, underwear, and stockings away in her bag, promising to return in the evening. Then silence fell on the house; not one of us felt like eating anything; it was still hot and everything was very strange. We let our large upstairs room to a certain Mr Goudsmit, a divorced man in his thirties, who appeared to have nothing to do on this particular evening; we simply could not get rid of him without being rude; he hung about until ten o'clock. At eleven o'clock Miep and Henk Van Santen arrived. Once again, shoes, stockings, books and underclothes disappeared into Miep's bag and Henk's deep pockets, and at eleven-thirty they too disappeared. I was dog-tired, and although I knew that it would be my last night in my own bed I fell asleep immediately and didn't wake up until Mummy called me at five-thirty the next morning. Luckily, it was not so hot as Sunday; warm rain fell steadily all day. We put on heaps of clothes as if we were going to the North Pole, the sole reason being to take clothes with us. No Jew in our situation would have dreamt of going out with a suitcase full of clothing. I had on two vests, three pairs of knickers, a dress, on top of that a skirt, jacket, summer coat, two pairs of stockings, lace-up shoes, woolly cap, scarf and still more; I was nearly stifled before we started, but no one inquired about that.

At seven-thirty the door closed behind us.

Continued tomorrow.

Yours, ANNE.

Saturday, 11th July 1942

Dear Kitty,

    Daddy, Mummy and Margot can't get used to the sound of the Westertoren clock yet, which tells us the time every quarter of an hour.

I can. I loved it from the start, and especially in the night it's like a faithful friend. I expect you will be interested to hear what if feels like to "disappear"; well, all I can say is that I don't know myself yet. I don't think I shall ever feel really at home in this house, but that does not mean that I loathe it here, it is more like being on holiday in a very peculiar boarding-house. Rather a mad idea, perhaps, but that is how it strikes me. The "Secret Annexe" is an ideal hiding-place. Although it leans to one side and is damp, you'd never find such a comfortable hiding-place anywhere in Amsterdam; no, perhaps not even in the whole of Holland. Our little room looked very bare at first with nothing on the walls; but thanks to Daddy who had brought my film-star collection and picture postcards on beforehand, and with the aid of paste-pot and brush, I have transformed the wall into one gigantic picture. This makes it look much more cheerful and, when the Van Daans come, we'll get some wood from the attic, and make a few little cupboards for the walls and other odds and ends to make it look more lively.

    There are some large business premises on the right of us, and on the left a furniture workshop: there is no one there after working hours but, even so, sounds could travel through the walls. We have forbidden Margot to cough at night although she has a bad cold, and make her swallow large doses of codeine. I am longing for Tuesday when the Van Daans arrive; it will be much more fun and not so quiet. It is the silence that frightens me so in the evenings and at night. I wish like anything that one of our protectors could sleep here at night. I can't tell you how oppressive it is *never* to be able to go outdoors, also I'm scared to death that we shall be discovered and shot. That is not exactly a pleasant prospect. We have to whisper and tread lightly during the day, otherwise, the people in the warehouse might hear us.

    Someone is calling me.

    Yours, ANNE.

Anne Frank from *The Diary of Anne Frank*
(Longman) ⇨

Glossary
Joodse Invalide: Jewish old people's institution
Westertoren clock: The clock of a nearby church

 Answer in sentences.

1   On what date did the Franks go into hiding? *(1 mark)*

2   At what time did they leave home? *(1 mark)*

3   Why was it "lucky" that it was cooler than the day before? *(1 mark)*

4   Why do you think that Anne had deliberately not been told where the hiding place was? *(1 mark)*

5   Anne was just thirteen years old when she wrote these extracts. (Her diary was given to her as a birthday present on 12 June.) What evidence is there in the passage to suggest that she was younger than Margot? *(2 marks)*

6   True or false? Write out the statements that are true. *(3 marks)*

   a) Miep had worked for Mr Frank for over twenty years.
   b) Anne called their hiding place "The Secret Annexe".
   **c) The Franks gave Miep and Henk the clothes and books that they
       didn't want.**
   d) The Franks and Van Daans planned to share the same hiding place.
   **e) Anne was the only member of the Frank family who liked hearing the
       Westertoren clock.**

7   According to Anne, no Jew in the same situation as her family would dream of going out with a suitcase full of clothes. Why not? Explain why this would have been a dangerous thing to do. *(1 mark)*

8   Look at the belongings that Anne packed in the satchel. She calls these some of her most "vital" possessions. What do they tell us about Anne as a person? *(3 marks)*

9   In what ways was Anne finding it difficult to adjust to being in hiding? *(2 marks)*

U N I T

7

The wishes of Savitri

The story that follows is a sacred story from the Hindu scriptures.

Savitri was the name of an Indian princess whose devotion to her husband went far beyond the realms of normal human experience. For she was prepared to fight with death itself to regain her love.

When she was eighteen, her father – the old king Ashwapati – suggested that she should marry, as was the custom. But Savitri gently declined.

"My dear father," she said. "I am not yet ready to marry. First let me travel for a year, praying at the shrines and listening to the words of the holy men so that I may draw closer to God."

"But Savitri," the king replied, "you are eighteen. You are of marrying age."

"I am young enough," Savitri laughed. "You'll see. If I am to be married, destiny will find me a husband."

And so it was. Savitri wandered for a year, meeting with holy men up and down the country. She ate the simplest food and slept under the stars. To meet her, none would have guessed that she was a princess, for she had left the fineries of palace life far behind her.

Eventually her travels brought her to a forest where she chanced to see a tall, handsome man carrying an axe in one hand and a bundle of firewood in the other. At first she thought he was nothing more than a huntsman or forester, but there was something about him – the nobility of his bearing perhaps – that made her think again. Despite the roughness of his clothes and the meanness of his occupation, she could not help but wonder if, like herself, he was not royally born, and out of sheer curiosity (or at least, she assured herself that it was only curiosity) she asked him to tell her about himself.

"Madam," the young man said, "my name is Satyavan. Once I lived in a great palace, surrounded by stewards and servants. My father was the king, but in his old age, he lost his sight. Then his courtiers were able to conspire against him and – alas that I was not old enough to defend him – he was overthrown and banished. Now we live in poverty, in a small cottage in the forest. It is a hard life ... not so much for me, but it is very hard for my poor father." ⟳

When Savitri returned to her own palace, the joy of her arrival turned to astonishment when she announced that she intended to marry, and dismay when the name of her fiancé was revealed. For there was in the palace a holy man called Narada who knew everything that there was to know.

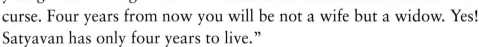

"You must not marry this Satyavan," he said.

"Why not?" Savitri asked.

"Because the unfortunate young man is living under a curse. Four years from now you will be not a wife but a widow. Yes! Satyavan has only four years to live."

When the princess heard this news her face went pale. But she had already plighted herself to Satyavan and did not intend to break her word.

And so the wedding was proclaimed. An iron ring was bound on Savitri's left wrist and her veil was tied to the cloak of Satyavan, as custom dictated. A sacred fire was lit and hand in hand they walked around it seven times while a priest chanted the ancient prayers. Then she put away all her jewels and fine clothes and went to live in the forest as the devoted wife of Satyavan and the dutiful daughter of his parents.

Never once did she tell her husband what Narada had foreseen, but never for a minute could she forget it. For it is often said in India that Yamaraja, the god of death, is the only god who never breaks his word and that if something is absolutely certain, then it is "as true as death". For this reason, Yamaraja is also known as the god of truth and of faith.

And after four years, he came.

Savitri and Satyavan were walking in the forest together when suddenly Satyavan stopped and complained that he was dizzy. A moment later he staggered. Suddenly cold with dread, Savitri ran to him, and she caught him just as he fell, fainting into her lap.

There was a rustle in the undergrowth. When Savitri looked up she saw a figure dressed in black, a noose of rough rope clasped in one hand. He looked at her with a sad expression and nodded. Then she knew that this was Yamaraja and that he had come for her husband.

"Savitri," he said, and his voice was strangely musical, like a song in a minor key. "I claim the soul of Satyavan as is my right. Do not be afraid for him. All his sorrows are now over."

He leant down and fastened the rope around the dying man's head. At the touch of the rope, the soul of Satyavan separated from his body, standing up to follow Yamaraja.

"Farewell," Yamaraja said. "And remember – I am the only god to whom everyone is faithful. One day you and I will meet again."

He turned and walked away but, driven by an instinct that made her forget her fear, Savitri followed. She followed him through the forest and into a second clearing where a waterfall splashed down into a rocky pool. Hearing her, Yamaraja turned again and now two black flames flickered where his eyes should have been, for his head had become a skull and his body, beneath the robes, a bare skeleton. But Savitri was not afraid.

"Still here!" Yamaraja exclaimed. "I see that you have more courage than sense, for who would willingly follow the god of death? Very well – I will give you a gift to help soothe your grief. You may ask for anything you like except for the life of your husband."

"Then I ask for my father-in-law's sight to be returned," Savitri said.

"It is granted," Yamaraja said. "Now farewell again."

For a second time, the god of death walked away, leading the soul of Satyavan behind him on the rope. Now the forest grew wild. Thistles sprang up and thorns pressed in on the path. Wild bats flitted in the air and owls hooted mysteriously in the shadows. But still Savitri followed, and when Yamaraja looked back, there she still was.

"I shall give you another wish," Yamaraja said, and now his voice was angry. "It is as much to dissuade you from this folly as to reward you for your devotion to your dead husband. But once again you may not ask for his life. Anything but that!"

"Then I would like my father-in-law's kingdom and his wealth to be returned to him," Savitri said.

"It is done. Now leave me!" ➪

But Savitri followed on. The forest grew ever darker and more savage. Now strange figures could be glimpsed gliding silently between the trees. A foul-smelling swamp bubbled nearby, tentacles of white mist spreading out over the ground.

"Still here!" exclaimed Yamaraja in all his fury when he turned round for a third time. "Never has a mortal so defied me! And a woman! A woman with the courage of ten men it would seem. Very well! One last wish will I grant you but then you and I must part company, lest I decide to keep you in my shadowy kingdom for all eternity. What will you have this time? So far you have favoured only your father-in-law. Now what can I give you for yourself?"

"Only this," Savitri said. "Grant that I may have many children and that I should live to see their children's children grow up in health and happiness. Will you give me this, great Yamaraja?"

"It is a good wish," Yamaraja said with a smile. "And I grant it."

Then it was Savitri's turn to smile. "You have forgotten," she said, "that according to Hindu law, a widow does not remarry."

Yamaraja thought for a moment, realising how he had been tricked. If Savitri could not remarry, then how could she have children and grandchildren? And yet that was what he had promised her, he who never broke his word. In which case ...

For a second, Savitri thought the god of death was going to strike her down where she stood, but then the forest rang with the sound of his laughter and he pulled the noose from around Satyavan's neck.

"It is a courageous woman who would follow her husband into the grave," he said. "And it is a cunning woman who would trick the god of death himself. Very well, Savitri, I will give you back the only man who can be the father of your children. And it will be a long, long time before the two of us meet again. Go in peace, for your devotion to Satyavan has defeated me."

Savitri and Satyavan returned to their cottage to discover that the sight and the fortunes of the old king had indeed been restored. And thus began a long and happy life in which the two were always true to one another. As true, indeed, as death.

Anthony Horowitz (retelling) adapted from *The Kingfisher Book of Myths and Legends* (Kingfisher)

 Answer in sentences.

1   How did destiny find a husband for Savitri? *(1.5 marks)*

2   What is the meaning of "declined" (paragraph two)? *(1 mark)*

3   Why was everyone at home dismayed to hear that it was Satyavan whom Savitri wanted to marry? *(1 mark)*

4   How long were Savitri and Satyavan married before the god of death came for him? *(1 mark)*

5   What is a noose and why did Yamaraja carry one? *(2 marks)*

6   What was Yamaraja's reason for giving Savitri her first wish? (Use your own words.) *(1 mark)*

7   What was Yamaraja's reason for giving Savitri her second wish? (Again, use your own words to explain.) *(2 marks)*

8   How did Savitri's third wish save her husband's life? *(2 marks)*

9   In what ways do you find Savitri a remarkable woman? *(2 marks)*

10 What words or phrases could replace the underlined words below?

    a) He was overthrown and <u>banished.</u> *(0.5 mark)*

    b) She had already <u>plighted</u> herself to Satyavan. *(0.5 mark)*

    c) "You and I must part company, <u>lest</u> I decide to keep you in my shadowy kingdom for all eternity." *(0.5 mark)*

UNIT 8

The Winslow boy

Cast:

RONNIE WINSLOW: *14 years old, cadet at the Royal Naval College, Osborne*

GRACE WINSLOW: *his mother*

ARTHUR WINSLOW: *his father*

CATHERINE WINSLOW: *his sister*

DICKIE WINSLOW: *his brother*

JOHN WATHERSTONE: *Catherine's fiancé*

DESMOND CURRY: *family friend, hopelessly in love with Catherine*

VIOLET: *the Winslows' parlourmaid*

Introduction

It is Sunday lunchtime in July in the early 1900s. Catherine and John have just become engaged and the family is celebrating.

(There is a general buzz of conversation. VIOLET takes round the tray of glasses.)

Arthur: Good. *(He takes a drink.)*

(Toasting) Catherine and John.

(All drink – CATHERINE and JOHN to each other. VIOLET lingers, smiling.) *(Seeing VIOLET)* Ah, Violet! We mustn't leave you out. You must join this toast.

Violet: Well – thank you, sir.

(ARTHUR pours her out a glass.)

Not too much, sir, please. Just a sip.

Arthur: Quite so. Your reluctance would be more convincing if I hadn't noticed you'd brought an extra glass –

Violet *(taking the glass from ARTHUR)*: Oh, I didn't bring it for myself, sir. I brought it for Master Ronnie – *(She extends her glass)* Miss Kate and Mr John. *(She takes a sip.)*

Arthur: You brought an extra glass for Master Ronnie, Violet?

Violet *(mistaking the bewilderment)*: Well – I thought you might allow him just a sip, sir. Just to drink the toast. He's that grown-up these days. *(DESMOND is staring gloomily into his glass. The others are frozen with apprehension.)*

Arthur: Master Ronnie isn't due back from Osborne until Tuesday, Violet.

Violet: Oh no, sir. He's back already. Came back unexpectedly this morning, all by himself.

Arthur: No, Violet. That isn't true. Someone has been playing a joke.

Violet: Well, I saw him in here with my own two eyes, sir, as large as life just before you came in from church – and then I heard Mrs Winslow talking to him in his room –

Arthur: Grace – what does this mean?

Catherine (*instinctively taking charge*): All right, Violet. You can go.

Violet: Yes, miss. (*VIOLET goes out.*)

Arthur (*to CATHERINE*): Did you know Ronnie was back?

Catherine: Yes.

Arthur: And you, Dickie?

Dickie: Yes, Father.

Arthur: Grace?

Grace (*helplessly*): We thought it best you shouldn't know – for the time being. Only for the time being, Arthur.

Arthur (*slowly*): Is the boy ill? (*No one answers. ARTHUR looks from one face to another in bewilderment.*)

Answer me, someone! Is the boy very ill? Why must I be kept in the dark like this? Surely I have the right to know. If he's ill I must be with him –

Catherine (*steadily*): No, Father. He's not ill.

(*ARTHUR suddenly realises the truth from the tone of her voice.*)

Arthur: Will someone tell me what has happened, please?

(*GRACE looks at CATHERINE with helpless enquiry. CATHERINE nods. GRACE takes the letter from her dress.*)

Grace (*timidly*): He brought this letter for you – Arthur.

Arthur: Read it to me, please –

Grace: Arthur – not in front of –

Arthur: Read it to me, please.

(*GRACE again looks at CATHERINE for advice, and again receives a nod. ARTHUR is sitting with his head bowed. GRACE begins to read.*)

Grace: "Confidential. I am commanded by My Lords Commissioners of the Admiralty to inform you that they have received a communication from the Commanding Officer of the Royal Naval College at Osborne, reporting the theft of a five shilling postal order at the College on the 7th instant, which was afterwards cashed at the post office. ⇨

Investigation of the circumstances of the case leaves no other conclusion possible than that the postal order was taken by your son, Cadet Ronald Arthur Winslow. My Lords deeply regret that they must therefore request you to withdraw your son from the College." It's signed by someone – I can't quite read his name –

(She turns away quickly to hide her tears. CATHERINE puts a comforting hand on her shoulder. ARTHUR has not changed his attitude. There is a pause. The gong sounds in the hall outside.)

Arthur (at length): Desmond – be so good as to call Violet.

(DESMOND goes into the hall. The gong stops. He returns at once and VIOLET enters.)

Violet, ask Master Ronnie to come down and see me.

Grace *(rising):* Arthur – he's in bed.

Arthur: You told me he wasn't ill.

Grace: He's not at all well.

Arthur: Do as I say, Violet.

Violet: Very good, sir. *(VIOLET goes out.)*

Arthur: Perhaps the rest of you would go in to luncheon? Grace, would you take them in?

Grace *(hovering):* Arthur – don't you think –

Arthur *(ignoring her):* Dickie, will you decant the bottle of claret I brought up from the cellar?

Dickie: Yes, Father.

Arthur: I put it on the sideboard in the dining-room.

Dickie: Yes, Father.

(DICKIE goes into the dining-room.)

Arthur: Will you go in, Desmond? And John? *(DESMOND and JOHN go into the dining-room. CATHERINE follows them to the door and waits. GRACE is still hovering.)*

Grace: Arthur?

Arthur: Yes, Grace?

Grace: Please don't – please don't – *(She stops, uncertainly.)*

Arthur: What mustn't I do?

Grace: Please don't forget he's only a child –

(ARTHUR does not answer her.)

Catherine: Come on, Mother.

(GRACE goes up to CATHERINE at the door. She looks back at ARTHUR. He has still not altered his position and is ignoring her. She

goes into the dining-room followed by CATHERINE. ARTHUR does not move after they are gone. After an appreciable pause there comes a timid knock on the hall door.)

Arthur: Come in.

(RONNIE appears in the doorway. He is in a dressing-gown. He stands on the threshold.)

Come in and shut the door. *(RONNIE closes the door behind him.)*

Come over here. *(RONNIE walks slowly up to his father. ARTHUR gazes at him steadily for some time, without speaking.)*

(At length.) Why aren't you in your uniform?

Ronnie *(murmuring):* It got wet.

Arthur: How did it get wet?

Ronnie: I was out in the garden in the rain.

Arthur: Why?

Ronnie *(reluctantly):* I was hiding.

Arthur: From me? *(RONNIE nods)*

Do you remember once, you promised me that if ever you were in trouble of any sort you would come to me first?

Ronnie: Yes, Father.

Arthur: Why didn't you come to me now? Why did you have to go and hide in the garden?

Ronnie: I don't know, Father.

Arthur: Are you so frightened of me?

(RONNIE does not reply. ARTHUR gazes at him for a moment, then holds up the letter.)

In this letter it says you stole a postal order.

(RONNIE opens his mouth to speak. ARTHUR stops him.)

Now I don't want you to say a word until you've heard what I've got to say. If you did it, you must tell me. I shan't be angry with you, Ronnie – provided you tell me the truth. But if you tell me a lie, I shall know it, because a lie between you and me can't be hidden. I shall know it, Ronnie – so remember that before you speak. *(He pauses.)* Did you steal this postal order?

Ronnie *(without hesitation):* No, Father. I didn't.

(ARTHUR takes a step towards him.)

Arthur *(staring into his eyes):* Did you steal this postal order?

Ronnie: No, Father. I didn't.

(ARTHUR continues to stare into his eyes for a second, then relaxes.) ⮕

Arthur: Go on back to bed. *(RONNIE goes gratefully to the hall door.)* And in future I trust that a son of mine will at least show enough sense to come out of the rain.

Ronnie: Yes, Father.

(RONNIE goes out. ARTHUR crosses to the desk. He picks up the telephone.)

Arthur *(into the telephone)*: Hullo. Are you there? *(He speaks very distinctly.)* I want to put a trunk call through, please. A trunk call ... Yes ... The Royal Naval College, Osborne ...

Terence Rattigan from *The Winslow Boy* (Nick Hern Books)

 Answer in sentences unless otherwise instructed.

1. Why is Desmond staring "gloomily" into his glass? *(1 mark)*

2. Why is Arthur surprised to hear that Violet has brought a glass for Ronnie? *(1 mark)*

3. Why has Ronnie been sent home before the end of term? *(1 mark)*

4. Why is Mrs Winslow reluctant to read aloud the letter Ronnie has brought with him? *(1 mark)*

5. Why do you think everyone is afraid of Mr Winslow? *(2 marks)*

6. Catherine tells John earlier in the play that her father "worships" Ronnie. What evidence is there in this extract that Mr Winslow loves Ronnie very much? *(2 marks)*

7. How does Mr Winslow satisfy himself that Ronnie is telling the truth? *(2 marks)*

8. Who do you think is the more decisive character, Catherine or her mother? Give your reasons. *(2 marks)*

9. Why do you think Mr Winslow is phoning the Royal Naval College? *(1 mark)*

10. Suggest words or phrases that could replace the underlined words in these stage directions:

    a) VIOLET lingers, smiling. (0.5 mark)
    b) She extends her glass. (0.5 mark)
    c) The others are frozen with apprehension. (0.5 mark)
    d) After an appreciable pause, there comes a timid knock. (0.5 mark)

Salt is special

Salt is one of the most valuable substances known to us. Plants and creatures, including human beings, need salt just to stay alive. Salt also prevents some foodstuffs going bad. It flavours food such as bread, butter and cheese; it softens hard water; it freezes ice cream.

In hospitals, refined salt is used in saline drips. These drip a weak solution of brine and liquid food through a hollow needle into a blood vessel in a patient's arm. Saline drips are used to feed patients too ill or weak to eat.

In countries with snowy winters, salt helps to keep roads clear of snow and ice. Special trucks, called gritters, scatter rock salt on the roads. The salt melts lying snow or ice, and stops more forming.

Salt plays an important part in the manufacture of clothes and household goods. Soaking animal skins and hides in brine prepares them for the tanning process that turns them into leather. Adding salt to a bath of dye "fixes" the dissolved colours on to the fabric being dyed. Adding salt to a paste of boiled oil, fats and caustic soda helps to turn it into soap. Salt is also used in water softeners. Here the sodium from salt replaces the dissolved magnesium and calcium that make some water so hard that soap will not form a lather. Water softeners also prevent a scaly crust forming in pipes and kettles.

More than four-fifths of all the salt produced is used in factories producing chemicals. Salt helps in the manufacture of about a dozen ⤷

chemicals used for making many hundreds of products. These range from adhesives, fertilisers, soap and toothpaste to synthetic rubber, and a material that whitens paper. All told we use salt in more than 15,000 ways.

At first people obtained salt mainly from the sea. Indeed salt gets its name from *sal,* a Latin word for salt that comes from *hals,* a Greek word meaning "sea".

Salt became one of the first products traded between one country and another. Bars of salt were carried from the coast to the inland cities of the Middle East. Arab merchants traded salt for precious goods such as jewels, silks and spices. One of Italy's oldest roads was built especially to carry salt. This road was called the *Via Salaria* (Salt Way), and ran from Ostia on the coast of Italy all the way to Rome.

Roman leaders partly paid their troops in salt. The Romans called this pay a *salarium,* from which we get the word "salary". Until recently, cakes of salt were used as money in parts of Africa and Asia.

People fought and died to win coasts rich in salt supplies. The Carthaginians and the Romans fought partly to control the Mediterranean salt-producing centres, as well as routes that carried salt and other goods. After their victory, the Romans ploughed salt into the soil of Carthage so no crops would grow there.

In the past, governments raised cash by imposing tax on the price of salt. For example, five hundred years ago the French king brought in a heavy salt tax known as the *gabelle,* which caused much hardship for the poor. The burden of this and other taxes was one reason why the French deposed their king in the French Revolution of 1789. Another example can be found during the time Britain ruled India. The British made the Indians pay a salt tax. Such laws were so unpopular that Mahatma Gandhi inspired many people to disobey them, which contributed to the end of British rule in India.

People prized salt long before most of its uses were discovered. Salt still comes from the sea, but huge amounts are also mined from underground. The salt you scatter on your plate is just a fraction of the 170 million tonnes or so the world consumes each year.

David Lambert adapted from *Focus on Salt* (Wayland)

1   Where do we get our supplies of salt from today? *(1 mark)*

2   How many tonnes of salt are consumed world-wide in a year? *(1 mark)*

3   Mention three different uses of salt in food production. *(3 marks)*

4   List three (non-food) products used today that required salt at some stage of their manufacture. *(3 marks)*

5   Why is salt used on icy roads? *(1 mark)*

6   What part does salt play in the treatment of some very sick patients? *(1 mark)*

7   Name two countries which once put a tax on salt. *(1 mark)*

8   What is salt mainly used for today? *(1 mark)*

    a) It is used for flavouring food like crisps.
    b) It is used for making roads in poor countries.
    c) It helps to raise taxes for schools and hospitals.
    d) It is used in the manufacture of chemicals.

9   What is the connection between salt and our modern word "salary"? *(1 mark)*

10   What do these words mean in the passage?

    a) brine (paragraph four) *(0.5 mark)*
    b) adhesives (paragraph five) *(0.5 mark)*
    c) synthetic (paragraph five) *(0.5 mark)*
    d) deposed (paragraph ten) *(0.5 mark)*

UNIT 10

Jane Eyre

Mr Lloyd has been called to see Jane, an orphan living with her aunt and cousins in Gateshead Hall.

In the course of the morning Mr Lloyd came up again.

"What, already up!" said he, as he entered the nursery. "Well, nurse, how is she?"

Bessie answered that I was doing very well.

"Then she ought to look more cheerful. Come here, Miss Jane: your name is Jane, is it not?"

"Yes, sir; Jane Eyre."

"Well, you have been crying, Miss Jane Eyre: can you tell me what about? Have you any pain?"

"No, sir."

"Oh! I dare say she is crying because she could not go out with missis in the carriage," interposed Bessie.

"Surely not! She is too old for such pettishness."

I thought so too; and my self-esteem being wounded by a false charge, I answered promptly, "I never cried for such a thing in my life: I hate going out in the carriage. I cry because I am miserable."

"Oh, fie, Miss!" said Bessie.

The good doctor appeared a little puzzled. I was standing before him: he fixed his eyes on me very steadily. "What made you ill yesterday?" he said.

"She had a fall," said Bessie, again putting in her word.

"Fall! why, that is like a baby again! Can't she manage to walk at her age? She must be eight or nine years old."

"I was knocked down," was the blunt explanation, jerked out of me by another pang of mortified pride; "but that did not make me ill," I added; while Mr Lloyd helped himself to a pinch of snuff.

As he was returning the box to his waistcoat pocket, a loud bell rang for the servants' dinner; he knew what it was. "That's for you, nurse," said he; "you can go down; I'll give Miss Jane a lecture till you come back."

Bessie would rather have stayed, but she was obliged to go, because punctuality at meals was rigidly enforced at Gateshead Hall.

"The fall did not make you ill; what did, then?" pursued Mr Lloyd, when Bessie had gone.

"I was shut up in a room where there is a ghost, till after dark."

I saw Mr Lloyd smile and frown at the same time: "Ghost! What, you are a baby after all! You are afraid of ghosts?"

"Of Mr Reed's ghost I am; he died in that room, and was laid out there. Neither Bessie nor anyone else will go into it at night, if they can help it; and it was cruel to shut me up alone without a candle – so cruel that I think I shall never forget it."

"Nonsense! And is it that makes you so miserable? Are you afraid now in daylight?"

"No: but night will come again before long; and besides, I am unhappy – very unhappy, for other things."

"What other things? Can you tell me some of them?"

How much I wished to reply fully to this question! How difficult it was to frame any answer! Children can feel, but they cannot analyse their feelings.

"For one thing, I have no father or mother, brothers or sisters."

"You have a kind aunt and cousins."

Again I paused. Then I said, "But John Reed knocked me down, and my aunt shut me up in the red-room."

Mr Lloyd a second time produced his snuff-box.

"Don't you think Gateshead Hall a very beautiful house?" asked he. "Are you not very thankful to have such a fine place to live at?"

"It is not my house, sir; and Abbot says I have less right to be here than a servant."

"Pooh! You can't be silly enough to wish to leave such a splendid place?"

"If I had anywhere else to go, I should be glad to leave it; but I can never get away from Gateshead till I am a woman."

"Perhaps you may – who knows? Have you any relation besides Mrs Reed?" ⇨

"I think not, sir."

"None belonging to your father?"

"I don't know: I asked Aunt Reed once, and she said possibly I might have some poor, low relations called Eyre, but she knew nothing about them."

"If you had such, would you like to go to them?"

"No: I should not like to belong to poor people," was my reply.

"But are your relatives so very poor? Are they working people?"

"I cannot tell; Aunt Reed says if I have any, they must be a beggarly set; I should not like to go a-begging."

"Would you like to go to school?"

"I should indeed like to go to school."

"Well, well; who knows what may happen?" said Mr Lloyd, as he got up. "The child ought to have a change of air and scene," he added, speaking to himself; "nerves not in a good state."

Bessie now returned; at the same moment the carriage was heard rolling up the gravel-walk.

"Is that your mistress, nurse?" asked Mr Lloyd. "I should like to speak to her before I go."

Bessie invited him to walk into the breakfast-room and led the way out. In the interview which followed between him and Mrs Reed, I presume, from after-occurrences, that Mr Lloyd ventured to recommend my being sent to school; and the recommendation was no doubt readily enough adopted; for as Abbot said, in discussing the subject with Bessie, when both sat sewing in the nursery one night after I was in bed, and, as they thought, asleep, "Missis was, she dared say, glad enough to get rid of such a tiresome ill-conditioned child, who always looked as if she were watching everybody, and scheming plots underhand."

On that same occasion I learned, for the first time, that my father had been a poor clergyman; that my mother had married him against the wishes of her friends, who considered the match beneath her; that my grandfather Reed was so irritated at her disobedience, he cut her off without a shilling; that after my parents had been married a year, my father caught the typhus fever while visiting the poor of a large manufacturing town and that my mother took the infection from him, and both died within a month of each other.

Bessie, when she heard this narrative, sighed and said, "Poor Miss Jane is to be pitied too, Abbot."

"Yes," responded Abbot; "if she were a nice, pretty child, one might pity her; but one really cannot care for such a little toad as that."

"Not a great deal, to be sure," agreed Bessie: "at any rate, a beauty like Miss Georgiana would be more moving in the same condition."

"Yes, I dote on Miss Georgiana!" cried the fervent Abbot. "Little darling! – with her long curls and her blue eyes, and such a sweet colour as she has; just as if she were painted! – Bessie, I could fancy a Welsh rabbit for supper."

"So could I – with a roast onion. Come, we'll go down." They went.

Charlotte Brontë adapted from *Jane Eyre* (Penguin)

 Choose the correct answer to each question and write it out.

1   What had made Jane ill? *(1.5 marks)*

   a) She had fallen over.
   b) She missed her uncle.
   c) She had been locked in a dark room.   C
   d) She had been knocked down.

2   Why didn't Jane live with her parents? *(1.5 marks)*

   a) She didn't like living with poor people.
   b) Her parents were dead.   B
   c) They had been cut off without a shilling.
   d) Her parents wanted her to live with her aunt.

3   What was Bessie's position in the household? *(1.5 marks)*

   a) She was the housemaid.
   b) She was the cook.
   c) She was the governess.   D
   d) She was the nursemaid.

4   What was the surname of Jane's mother before she married? *(1.5 marks)*

   a) Lloyd
   b) Eyre   B
   c) Reed
   d) Brontë

5   What did Abbot mean when she described Jane as "a little toad"? *(1.5 marks)*

a) She meant that Jane was ugly.
b) She meant that Jane's nose was always running.
c) She meant that Jane was badly behaved.
d) She meant that Jane hated being indoors.

6   Why was Mr Lloyd pleased when Bessie had to go to the servants' hall for dinner? *(1.5 marks)*

a) He knew that Bessie was hungry.
b) He wanted to question Jane without being interrupted.
c) Bessie made him nervous.
d) He couldn't understand what Bessie said.

7   Why did the friends and family of Jane's mother disapprove of the man she married? *(1.5 marks)*

a) He was not a nice person.
b) He was out of work.
c) He was much older than she was.
d) He was not rich enough.

8   Why did Mr Lloyd think it might be a good idea for Jane to go away to school? *(1.5 marks)*

a) He thought she was backward for her age.
b) He thought she should get away from Gateshead Hall.
c) He thought girls should have as good an education as boys.
d) He knew Mrs Reed would be pleased.

9   Why did Mr Lloyd want to see Mrs Reed before he went? *(1.5 marks)*

a) He wanted to suggest that Jane went to school.
b) He wanted to tell her what he thought of her.
c) He wanted to be paid.
d) He wanted to check that Mrs Reed was well.

10   Why did Bessie and Abbot feel sure that Mrs Reed would let Jane go away to school? *(1.5 marks)*

a) They knew she would be glad to get Jane out of the house.
b) They knew how generous she was.
c) They knew how much she approved of a private education.
d) They knew that she had been thinking about it for a long time.

Tell me about your dream

"It's always the same you see,
Never varies, and always
Leaves me sweating with fright.
Talk you through it?
Well, I'll try.
Yes, that's right, I'm at a football match,
And it's a big game, really big.
We're all waiting,
Waiting for the teams to emerge.
Then suddenly over the speakers
The voice comes, very clear,
And everybody goes quiet.
Do I remember what it says?
Well yes; two of the players
Have missed the train
So they're a man short, it says,
And if anyone
Happens to have his boots
They'd be grateful if he'll play.
Course I have,
Always bring my boots
Because I know from my dream
This could happen.
What? That's right,
I don't know if it's a dream or not.
In a flash I'm over the fence
And suddenly I'm in the dressing room
Surrounded by famous players
All shaking my hand
And clapping me on the back.
As they run out
The manager holds me back.
He looks me in the eye and says,
'I've kept you back
To appoint you captain.
I want you out last
To enjoy alone your moment of glory.' ⇨

45

He hands me a number nine shirt.
'Wear it with pride lad';
And then I'm off
Up the dark tunnel
To my moment of glory.
My studs rattle on the concrete
And the crowd's roar
Is like a great beast
Breathing far away.
I run down a white corridor
Now they're calling my name
Soon I'll trot out into the sun.
Suddenly I come to a wall.
I don't know whether to go left or right.
I take the right one
But the right one
Turns out to be the wrong one.
It leads to another white corridor
And another white corridor
And another white corridor;
The crowd's far away now
And I'm hopelessly lost
And suddenly I wake up
Shaking with fright.
That's it.
What have I done about it?
Well, I don't take my boots
To matches any more because,
Well, you never know.
Has it helped to talk about it?
Yes, I suppose it has.
Do I want to ask any questions?
Well, there is one thing.
I don't know if you can tell me:
Is this a dream?"

Gareth Owen from *Another Fourth
Poetry Book*, ed. John Foster
(Oxford University Press)

1   Who do you think is saying the words, "Tell me about your dream"? *(1 mark)*
   a) a friend
   b) a football manager
   c) a counsellor or therapist
   d) a newspaper reporter

2   Why is only one volunteer needed if two players have missed the train? *(1 mark)*

3   Why does the manager hold the dreamer back when the other players leave the dressing room? *(1 mark)*

4   What makes the dream so frightening that the dreamer always wakes up "sweating with fright"? *(2 marks)*

5   We can deduce that the speaker is asked a number of questions as he relates his dream. List four of the questions put to him. *(2 marks)*

6   What steps has the speaker taken to ensure that this dream never becomes reality? *(1 mark)*

7   How old do you think the speaker is? Give your reasons. *(2 marks)*

8   Explain what fear lies behind the last line of the poem. *(1 mark)*

9   How does Gareth Owen make the dream convincingly dreamlike? Give at least three points. *(3 marks)*

10   Why do you think this poem will appeal to a lot of readers, whether they are interested in football or not? *(1 mark)*

UNIT 12

Romeo meets Juliet

In old Verona, where the streets were hot and narrow and the walls were high, where men were as bright as wasps and carried quick swords for their stings, there lived two families – the Capulets and the Montagues – who hated each other worse than death. They had but to pass in the street and they were at each other's throats like dogs in the sun. Cursing and shouting and bawling, and crashing from civil pillar to post, they filled the good people of Verona with fear and anger to have their city's peace so senselessly disturbed.

They were at it again! In the buzzing heat of a July morning, two lazy no-good servants of the Capulets had spied two strolling men of the Montagues. Looks had been exchanged, then words, and in moments the peaceful market was in an uproar as the four idle ruffians set about defending their masters' honour by smashing up stalls, overturning baskets, wrecking shops and wounding passers-by, in their valiant endeavours to cut each other into pieces.

Benvolio, a sensible young Montague, came upon the scene and tried to put a stop to it; Tybalt, a young Capulet so full of fury that he sweated knives, promptly went for Benvolio; old Montague and old Capulet appeared and tried to draw their doddering swords – that surely would have shaken more like straws in the wind than lightning in the sky. Men shouted, women screamed and rushed to drag wandering infants into safety ... and bloody riot threatened to swallow up all the fair city, till the Prince of Verona, with soldiers, came furiously into the square.

"Rebellious subjects, enemies to peace!" he roared; and, by dint of stern anger and sterner threats, restored some semblance of peace. The vile destructive brawling between the Montagues and the Capulets incensed him beyond measure.

"If ever you disturb our streets again," he swore, "your lives shall pay the forfeit."

When the Prince had gone, taking old Capulet with him (to remove one half of the quarrel and so leave the other without an object), Lady Montague spoke to Benvolio.

"O where is Romeo, saw you him today?" she asked. "Right glad I am he was not at this fray," she added, as if Romeo, her only son, who was as hot-headed as any, would surely have come to grief among the flashing swords and blundering fists. But Romeo had been elsewhere,

wrapped in a melancholy that was most mysterious to his parents.

"See where he comes!" exclaimed Benvolio, as the young man in question drifted dolefully into the square, as if he was a ghost under instruction to haunt it. "So please you step aside," he urged old Montague and his wife. "I'll know his grievance ..."

The parents departed, leaving Benvolio to penetrate the inscrutable mystery of his cousin Romeo's gloom. It proved no great task, as Romeo was all too willing to talk. He was in love. Hopelessly. He doted to distraction upon a glorious creature by the name of Rosalyne; and she would have nothing to do with him. So far as she was concerned, he was dust. Consequently he had been mooning all morning, lovesick, in a grove of sycamores.

Patiently Benvolio listened to the extensive catalogue of Rosalyne's amazing charms. He shook his head, and ventured to suggest that, if only Romeo looked about him, he might find others as fair. Impossible! The world was not so rich as to hold another such as Rosalyne. Benvolio expressed doubts, but Romeo was adamant; and so they continued, strolling through the golden warm streets of Verona, Romeo all melancholy passion and Benvolio all cheerful good sense.

"Why, Romeo, art thou mad?" began Benvolio when a serving man, much bewildered, and with a paper in his hand, accosted them.

"I pray, sir, can you read?" ⇨

It seemed the fellow's master had entrusted him with a list of guests to be invited to a banquet that night. But, being no scholar, he could make neither head nor tail of the writing. Obligingly, Romeo read out the names. They were a distinguished company – and among them was Rosalyne!

Where was the feast to be? Alas! at the house of old Capulet. A dangerous place for a Montague. But, if he went masked and in fantastical costume, as was the custom for uninvited guests at such a feast...

"Go thither," urged Benvolio, anxious to cure his cousin of that sickness called Rosalyne. He had noticed that on the list had been the best beauties of Verona, beside whom Rosalyne might well not shine so bright. "Compare her face," he advised shrewdly, "with some that I shall show; and I will make thee think thy swan a crow."

They met that night in the street outside the Capulets' house: Romeo, Benvolio and Mercutio, who was a kinsman of the Prince and Romeo's dearest friend. He was a lively, mocking youth, as full of bubbling laughter as a glass of good wine. They met by torchlight with some half dozen others, all in fantastical costume and gilded masks – as if King Midas had patted their heads and made fortunes of their faces.

Like gorgeous dragonflies, with partly folded wings, they leaned against the high wall that enclosed the Capulets' orchard, laughing and talking and trying, by all manner and means, to lift up Romeo's depressed spirits. Neither Benvolio's urging nor Mercutio's wit affected him. He stayed glum; and furthermore, had had a strange premonition that the night's festivities would turn out to have been the beginning of a journey to the grave.

At length the maskers gave up their efforts and, with their gloomy companion, went into the feasting house. At once they were dazzled by a blaze of candles and a blaze of beauty ... of silks and satins, soft white skin and dark, delighted eyes.

"You are welcome, gentlemen!" cried old Capulet, in holiday robes and cheerful to see so fine a company of maskers at his feast.

"Come, musicians, play. A hall, a hall, give room! And foot it, girls!"

Music scraped and set a pulse, and the dancing began. Gowns rustled, filling the air with perfume; buckled shoes, like bright mice, twinkled in and out of richly swinging hems; fingers touched, hands entwined; masks and faces bobbed and turned, exchanging silver looks for golden smiles.

All were dancing, but Romeo. He stood, marble pilgrim, stock-still and amazed! At last he spoke, to a servant standing by.

"What lady's that which doth enrich the hand of yonder knight?"

"I know not, sir," returned the servant.

"O she doth teach the torches to burn bright!" breathed Romeo, as he gazed at the girl whose beauty had, in an instant, overturned his heart.

Leon Garfield from *Shakespeare Stories* (Gollancz Children's Paperbacks)

Answer in sentences.

1   Explain how the brawling between the young men was "destructive". *(1.5 marks)*

2   In the first sentence, the men of Verona are described as being "as bright as wasps". Explain. *(1 mark)*

3   How did Benvolio get involved in the fighting? *(1 mark)*

4   Explain in your own words the ultimatum the Prince issued to the Capulets and Montagues. *(1 mark)*

5   Write out the statements that are true: *(1.5 marks)*

    a) Romeo had no brothers.   **b) Romeo lived in Verona.**
    c) Romeo and Benvolio were cousins.   **d) Romeo and Rosalyne were in love.**

6   Put these words spoken by Lady Montague into clear, modern English:
    "O where is Romeo, saw you him today? Right glad I am he was not at
    this fray." *(1 mark)*

7   Why did Benvolio suggest to Romeo's parents that they leave him alone
    with Romeo for a while? *(0.5 mark)*

8   Look at paragraph nine, beginning "The parents departed ...". Suggest words
    or phrases that could replace these:

    a) departed *(0.5 mark)*   **b) gloom** *(0.5 mark)*
    c) doted to distraction upon *(0.5 mark)*   **d) consequently** *(0.5 mark)*

9   How did Romeo find out that Rosalyne would be at the Capulets' banquet?
    (0.5 mark)

10 Give two reasons why Romeo and his friends were masked and in fancy dress
    at the banquet. *(1 mark)*

11 Romeo had a "premonition" before entering the Capulets' house and seeing
    Juliet for the first time. What is a "premonition"? *(1 mark)*

12 It seems strange that the servant didn't know who Juliet was when Romeo
    questioned him. Why do you think he might not have known? *(1 mark)*

13 Benvolio is described as "a sensible young Montague". In what ways did he
    appear sensible in this extract? *(2 marks)*

The friends

*"Monkey-chaser" and "teacher's pet" – that's what the children in her
new school call Phyllisia. They don't like her because she's an outsider.
She comes from the West Indies, speaks with a different accent, and can
answer more questions in class. Then comes the dreadful day when nearly
all the class gang up on her and wait for her after school. They attack her
and she is terrified. She feels angry and frustrated, and tries to explain the
situation to her mother. Her sister Ruby has found her own way of
dealing with the bullies, but Phyllisia is reluctant to take her advice.*

Rushing into the apartment, planning
to hide in my room, I ran right into my
mother's arms. *"Bon Dieu,"* she cried
after one look at my face. "What is this?
What have they done to you?"

The look of my mother – tall, and
with an olive complexion with black,
black eyes – has always awed me. As I saw
her now, heard her voice, rich, deep,
softened by the French Creole of The
Island – it tickled the pores of my skin,
thickened my throat with unshed tears
and jumbled my words as they fell thick
and heavy from my swollen lips.

"Al – all the chi – child – ren bunch up
and wa – ant to fi – fight me."

"Want to? From the look of your face
I would say they did fight you." She called
to my sister. "Ruby, Ruby, bring me a
basin of water and a rag."

Then pulling me into the living room,
she sat on the couch holding me to her
knees. "Tell me, Phyllisia, why? Don't the
children like you?"

The pity in her voice pushed me to the
brink of hysterics. "No. They hate me!
Everybody hates me!" ▷

"But how so?"

"I an – swer the que – questions the teach – er asks and – and the gi – girl be – hind says that I – I'm teacher's pet. And wh – hen I co – me down – stairs th – they all stand around wait – ing ..."

"How long has this been going on?"

"Si – ince the be – begin – ning. They say all ki – kinds of nas – ty things to – to me."

"Nasty things like what?"

"They – they call me mon – monkey chaser."

Ruby had come into the room with the basin of water. Mother turned to her: "Do you have trouble like this, Ruby?"

"No, Mother."

"Why is that? Is it because the children are older in your school?"

"It's because I don't stick my hand in the air all the time and try to prove how smart I am." Ruby spoke in her usual vain, airy manner. "After all, Mother, you know how Phyllisia is. If she did not try to act so smart and know-it-all, she would not be opening up her mouth and continually be reminding the children where she comes from."

All of my self-pity turned into a need for revenge. But I held myself at Mother's knees not to rush up and scratch at her pretty face.

Mother's eyes had widened. A pulse beat rapidly at her delicate throat. "Ruby, are you standing there telling me that you do not answer questions in class because you are ashamed of where you come from?"

Ruby did not notice the reproach in Mother's voice and went on in the same manner, "Well, the children don't like it and the teachers don't demand it, so why call attention to oneself? Sometimes when the children don't know the answer, I even slip it to them."

Aghast, Mother cried: "Is so? For shame, for shame, Ruby. I did not know that you were ashamed of yourself."

"I am not ashamed of myself, Mother." Ruby hated to be scolded. Tears rose quickly to her eyes. "But I want people to like me."

"Ruby, you are a nice-looking girl. You are well-mannered. If you can also add intelligence to that list, then you must look elsewhere for the reasons people don't like you."

Mother's displeasure gave me new confidence. "Mother," I pleaded, "I don't want to go back to that school tomorrow. Please, don't make me go back to that school."

"You have to go," she said quietly. "You are a West Indian girl going to school in New York and you are proud. What happens in this school will happen in any other. So if you must fight, you must."

For a moment I just stared. Did she know what it was to have a yelling mob ready to pounce on you? Or to have someone as tough as Beulah hate you for nothing? And to know that she would be waiting for you the next day? I thrust my swollen face angrily near to hers. "I don't bargain with my intelligence, but I don't want to be killed for it either."

"Oh, they will not kill you." I felt her withdrawing into that calm where nothing could reach her.

Usually I admired this "haughtiness". I often imitated it when I played the role of "grand lady". Now, however, I wanted to snatch at the calm, shock her into an anger to equal mine. How dare she sit there – inside of herself – and state that I would not be killed!

"I can't fight them all," I shouted. "I can't fight a bunch of ragamuffins whom I never did anything to and who hate me."

"They don't hate you, Phyllisia. They are probably full of resentment. And who would not be resentful in a city so tense, so oppressive as New York? But they don't hate you."

Stifling the urge to throw myself on the floor, to kick, to scream, have a tantrum, I screeched instead, "But it's me they're fighting!"

She smiled condescendingly. "You *are* a smart girl, Phyllisia, so try to understand. The children pick on you because you are still strange to them. But this time will pass. You wait and see. The children you are fighting today will be your friends tomorrow."

"I don't want to be their friend," I shrieked. "Never, never, do you hear? I don't want them to like me! I don't want to like them ..."

Rosa Guy from *The Friends* (Penguin)

1   "Al – all the chi – child – ren bunch up and wa – ant to fi – fight me."
     Why are Phyllisia's words printed in this broken-up way? *(1 mark)*

2   How did her mother feel when Phyllisia told her she was being bullied? *(1 mark)*

3   Why did hearing her mother's voice and accent make Phyllisia want to cry? *(1 mark)*

4   Why were the girls bullying her, according to Phyllisia? *(1 mark)*

5   Why were the girls bullying Phyllisia, according to her mother? *(1 mark)*

6   What different forms was the bullying taking? *(1 mark)*

7   Why wouldn't her mother let her leave the school and go to another one? *(2 marks)*

8   Give two reasons why Ruby deliberately said as little as possible in class. *(1 mark)*

9   Was "being liked" equally important to both girls? Give reasons for
     your answer. *(2 marks)*

10   Suggest words or phrases which could take the place of the words
     underlined below:

     a) Ruby did not notice the <u>reproach</u> in Mother's voice. *(1 mark)*

     b) <u>Aghast</u>, Mother cried: "Is so? For shame, for shame, Ruby." *(1 mark)*

     c) <u>Stifling</u> the urge to throw myself on the floor, to kick, to scream, have
        a tantrum, I screeched instead, "But it's me they're fighting." *(1 mark)*

     d) She smiled <u>condescendingly</u>. *(1 mark)*

Two ways of looking at a daffodil

When we are very young, the world, nature, people
are mysterious to us. Give a baby an orange. The baby
stares at it, fingers it, dribbles on it, drops it, howls
for you to pick it up again. It seems to be a beautiful,
round, coloured object, with a strange smell, which is
heavy to hold and stays put on the floor when dropped,
instead of walking away like a cat. A baby uses all five
senses to make such discoveries: like an explorer in a
new world, full of wonder and surprise at the novelty
of everything. In a way, a poet is someone who never
grows out of that sense of wonder. It keeps the
imagination constantly on the stretch and quivering at
the mysteriousness and beauty of the world; and thus
poetry helps *us* to understand the world by sharpening
our own senses, by making us more sensitive to life.

Now there are two ways of getting to understand
the world – through our heads and through our hearts,
our feelings. Science tells us a great deal about how the
world works, what it is made of, and so on. Science is
the chief way of learning through our heads. But that's
not the *only* way of learning about the world –
perhaps not even the best way. Let's take a very
ordinary object, the common wild daffodil. Here are
two ways of describing it:

(1) *Narcissus pseudo-narcissus: flower-stalk*
    hollow, two-edged, bearing near its summit
  a membranous sheath and a single flower:
  nectary notched and curled at the margin,
  as long as the sepals and petals.

(2) *I wandered lonely as a cloud,*
  That floats on high o'er vales and hills,
  When all at once I saw a crowd,
  A host of golden daffodils:
  Beside the lake, beneath the trees,
  Fluttering and dancing in the breeze. ⤵

Now, which do you think is the more satisfactory description of daffodils – the scientific one which I have taken from a text book on botany, or the poetic one which comes from a poem by Wordsworth? Of course, it's not quite fair to compare a scientific description with a poetic one like this, as though they were competing against each other for a prize. Science is concerned with finding out and stating the facts: poetry's task is to give you the look, the smell, the taste, the "feel" of those facts. Each has its own purpose and reward. But, by contrasting these two descriptions, you can see how poetry and science differ in method. Description (1) is analytic: that is to say, it examines the daffodil as though it was a single object quite separate from every other object which presents itself to our senses, tells us how it is composed, and classifies it. Description (2) relates the daffodils with a number of other things – with trees, a lake, a breeze, and with the poet's feeling of loneliness (at least, he was "lonely as a cloud" until he met this "host of golden daffodils").

It is the inclusion of *feeling* that makes the difference between poetry and science. Science is not concerned merely with analysing things: it also must try to relate them with each other and thus discover the natural laws at work behind them. But scientists use theory, observation and experiment to relate facts with each other, whereas poets use their own feelings, their emotions. It would be all wrong for a scientist to get emotional when describing a daffodil; and it would be all wrong for a poet *not* to.

There, then, is the great use of poetry. It tells us about the world through our feelings. It sharpens our senses, makes us more keenly and fully aware of life, exercises our imagination and stores up treasure in our memory: once we have seen that "host of golden daffodils" coloured by the poet's feeling, they will continue for the rest of our lives to "flash upon that inward eye which is the bliss of solitude".

Imagine, for a moment, that you are trying to describe one of your friends. It wouldn't be difficult to give the sort of description you hear on the radio when someone has disappeared from home or the police are after them. You could say the friend is tall, has blue eyes, a mole on the left cheek, a wooden leg or a red nose.

But that would only describe the *outside* of this person. It wouldn't tell people what your friend is really like – the habits, feelings, all the little peculiarities that make this person what he or she is and different from everyone else. You would find it very difficult indeed to describe the *inside* of your friend, even though you feel you know such a great friend through and through. Now good poetry *does* describe life in that way; it tells us about its inside as well as its outside, and thus it helps you to know and love the world as intimately as you know and love a friend.

C. Day Lewis adapted from *Poetry for You*
(Basil Blackwell)

 Answer in sentences.

1   Why does C. Day Lewis bother to mention the baby? *(1 mark)*

2   Which senses is the baby using while exploring the mysterious orange? *(3 marks)*

3   What is a "sense of wonder"? *(1 mark)*

4   In the poem referred to, the daffodils are described as "fluttering and dancing". How can daffodils "flutter" and "dance"? *(1 mark)*

5   Which of the two descriptions of the wild daffodils do you prefer, or do you find them both equally interesting? Give your reasons as clearly as you can. *(1 mark)*

6   True or false? Write the statements that are true: *(3 marks)*

   a) Scientists want to find out the facts.
   b) Scientists don't get excited about their work.
   c) Scientists investigate the world around them.
   d) Scientists want to make connections between things.
   e) Scientists aren't interested in poetry.

7   In what ways can a poet "sharpen" our senses? *(1 mark)*

8   What is the meaning of "novelty" (paragraph one)? *(1 mark)*

9   What is meant by "peculiarities" in the last paragraph? *(2 marks)*

10   Do you think that "Two ways of looking at a daffodil" is a good title for this passage? Give reasons for your response. *(1 mark)*

UNIT 15

The highwayman

Part one

The wind was a torrent of darkness among the gusty trees,
The moon was a ghostly galleon tossed upon cloudy seas,
The road was a ribbon of moonlight over the purple moor,
And the highwayman came riding –
    Riding – riding –
The highwayman came riding, up to the old inn-door.

He'd a French cocked-hat on his forehead, a bunch of lace at his chin,
A coat of the claret velvet, and breeches of brown doe-skin:
They fitted with never a wrinkle; his boots were up to the thigh!
And he rode with a jewelled twinkle,
    His pistol butts a-twinkle,
His rapier hilt a-twinkle, under the jewelled sky.

Over the cobbles he clattered and clashed in the dark inn-yard,
And he tapped with his whip on the shutters, but all was locked and
barred:
He whistled a tune to the window; and who should be waiting there
But the landlord's black-eyed daughter,
    Bess, the landlord's daughter,
Plaiting a dark red love-knot into her long black hair.

And dark in the dark old inn-yard a stable-wicket creaked
Where Tim, the ostler, listened; his face was white and peaked,
His eyes were hollows of madness, his hair like mouldy hay;
But he loved the landlord's daughter,
    The landlord's red-lipped daughter:
Dumb as a dog he listened, and he heard the robber say –

60

"One kiss, my bonny sweetheart, I'm after a prize tonight,
But I shall be back with the yellow gold before the morning light.
Yet if they press me sharply, and harry me through the day,
Then look for me by moonlight,
    Watch for me by moonlight:
I'll come to thee by moonlight, though hell should bar the way."

He rose upright in the stirrups, he scarce could reach her hand;
But she loosened her hair i' the casement! His face burnt like a brand
As the black cascade of perfume came tumbling over his breast;
And he kissed its waves in the moonlight,
    (Oh, sweet black waves in the moonlight)
Then he tugged at his reins in the moonlight, and galloped away to the
West.

Part two

He did not come in the dawning, he did not come at noon;
And out of the tawny sunset, before the rise o' the moon,
When the road was a gipsy's ribbon, looping the purple moor,
A red-coat troop came marching –
    Marching – marching –
King George's men came marching, up to the old inn-door.

They said no word to the landlord, they drank his ale instead;
But they gagged his daughter and bound her to the foot of her narrow bed.
Two of them knelt at her casement, with muskets at their side!
There was death at every window;
    And hell at one dark window;
For Bess could see, through her casement, the road that he would ride.

They had tied her up to attention, with many a sniggering jest:
They had bound a musket beside her, with the barrel beneath her breast!
"Now keep good watch!" and they kissed her.
    She heard the dead man say –
Look for me by moonlight;
    Watch for me by moonlight;
I'll come to thee by moonlight, though hell should bar the way! ▷

61

She twisted her hands behind her; but all the knots held good!
She writhed her hands till her fingers were wet with sweat or blood!
They stretched and strained in the darkness, and the hours crawled by like years
Till, now, on the stroke of midnight,
  Cold, on the stroke of midnight,
The tip of one finger touched it! The trigger at least was hers!

The tip of one finger touched it; she strove no more for the rest!
Up she stood to attention, with the barrel beneath her breast,
She would not risk their hearing: she would not strive again;
For the road lay bare in the moonlight,
  Blank and bare in the moonlight;
And the blood of her veins in the moonlight throbbed to her Love's refrain.

Tlot-tlot, tlot-tlot! Had they heard it? The horse-hoofs ringing clear –
Tlot-tlot, tlot-tlot, in the distance! Were they deaf that they did not hear?
Down the ribbon of moonlight, over the brow of the hill,
The highwayman came riding,
  Riding, riding!
The red-coats looked to their priming! She stood up straight and still!

Tlot-tlot, in the frosty silence! *Tlot-tlot*, in the echoing night!
Nearer he came and nearer! Her face was like a light!
Her eyes grew wide for a moment; she drew one last deep breath,
Then her finger moved in the moonlight;
  Her musket shattered the moonlight,
Shattered her breast in the moonlight and warned him – with her death.

He turned; he spurred to the westward; he did not know who stood
Bowed with her head o'er the musket, drenched with her own red blood!
Not till the dawn he heard it, and his face grew grey to hear
How, Bess, the landlord's daughter,
  The landlord's black-eyed daughter,
Had watched for her Love in the moonlight: and died in the darkness there.

Back, he spurred like a madman, shrieking a curse to the sky,
With the white road smoking behind him, and his rapier brandished high!
Blood-red were his spurs i' the golden noon; wine-red was his velvet coat;
When they shot him down on the highway,
  Down like a dog on the highway,
And he lay in his blood on the highway, with the bunch of lace at his throat.

Part three

And still of a winter's night, they say, when the wind is in the trees,
When the moon is a ghostly galleon tossed upon cloudy seas,
When the road is a ribbon of moonlight over the purple moor,
A highwayman comes riding –
  Riding – riding –
A highwayman comes riding, up to the old inn door.

Over the cobbles he clatters and clangs in the dark inn-yard;
And he taps with his whip on the shutters, but all is locked and barred:
He whistles a tune to the window, and who should be waiting there
But the landlord's black-eyed daughter,
  Bess, the landlord's daughter,
Plaiting a dark red love-knot into her long black hair.

Alfred Noyes from *The New Dragon Book of Verse*, ed. *Michael Harrison and Christopher Stuart-Clark*
(Oxford University Press)

Glossary
brand: the mark burned on to cattle to show who owns them
ostler: someone who looked after travellers' horses
musket: a gun with a long, thick barrel, used before rifles were invented ⇨

Answer in sentences.

1   What makes the moon look like a "ghostly galleon"? *(1 mark)*

2   Why is "ribbon" a good way of describing the road across the moor? *(1 mark)*

3   Say these lines to yourself:
    "And the highwayman came riding –
         Riding – riding
    The highwayman came riding, up to the old inn-door".
    Do you like the repetition of "riding"? What does it suggest about the
    highwayman and his journey? *(1 mark)*

4   Which word in verse two tells us that the night sky is full of stars? *(1 mark)*

5   Find the two verbs in verse three which describe the noise made by the hoofs
    of the highwayman's horse when he rides into the inn-yard over the cobbles.
    (1 mark)

6   Why is Tim jealous? *(1 mark)*

7   What colour is Tim's hair and how would it feel if it's like "mouldy hay"? *(1 mark)*

8   A "cascade" is a waterfall. How is Bess's hair just like a waterfall for a few
    seconds? *(1 mark)*

9   Why is the highwayman in a hurry and when does he promise to return? *(1 mark)*

10 Can you guess what Tim does now that he knows the highwayman's plans?
    (1 mark)

11 Why is the highwayman called "the dead man" (in Part two, verse three) when
    he is not dead? *(2 marks)*

12 How does Bess try to save the highwayman from being captured by King
    George's men? *(1 mark)*

13 Do you think the poem has a happy or a sad ending? Give your reasons. *(2 marks)*

Twist of gold

"Twist of gold" is set in Ireland over 150 years ago, during the Potato Famine in 1847. The Irish suffered terribly and thousands starved to death. As a result, they were suspicious of other people, especially those who were better off. This extract tells of an encounter between a poor boy and a soldier.

The boy and the Dragoon sat in the warm drizzle on either side of the river. It was a close, still evening and the flies were down. The boy knew he was there but ignored him as he had been instructed so often by his mother. He baited his hook yet again and cast it into the river. The Dragoon's horse stood with his legs in the cool of the water and drank tidily. The man sensed the boy's burning enmity; he had encountered it often enough before from the children in Ireland, but it hurt him nonetheless as it always did. He removed his heavy plumed helmet and placed it on the ground beside him, balancing it against the bank. His scarlet cloak he threw aside on the ground beside him and then lay back on it, his head resting on his hands, looking over the top of his boots at the boy who sat rock-still on the bank opposite him. This way, he thought, he could pretend to be asleep and watch the boy at the same time.

The boy wore nothing but rags, like all the other children, and he went bare-foot. He was thin, but not yet as skeletal as some the Dragoon had seen. The signs of hunger were there already, the hollow cheeks, the stick-like legs and the dreadful white of the bones at the knees. It was the child's sunken eyes though that held the Dragoon's attention, fixed as they were in complete concentration at the point where his line lay in the water. His whole body was taut and waiting behind those eyes. "It's as if his life depended on it," the Dragoon thought. And then, as he watched, the truth dawned on him in all its clarity. "For Christ's sake, Will," he said to himself, "what are you saying? His life does depend on it. Look at him. You're looking at a dead child. In a couple of weeks, in a couple of months, you'll be trotting along some dripping, leafy lane and you'll see a body lying muddy and still in a ditch. And it won't be just anybody's body, it'll be him." Impulse took him against his better judgement. The Dragoon sat up suddenly, resting on his elbows, and called out. ⇨

"Son, hey son!" The boy looked up slowly, his face full of smouldering resentment. "Son, I've some biscuits in my saddle bag. Would you like a biscuit, son? You'll not be catching any fish here, you know. I've been trying for weeks myself. The odd tiddly trout, that's all. Water too low. You'll not catch anything, not in a month of Sundays. There's eels of course, but it's too light for eels and too early." The boy glared at him as he spoke, his instinctive hatred mellowed already by the humanity in the man's voice. The Dragoon lowered his voice, deliberately trying to remove the threat from it. "Look, son. I won't hurt you. Honest, I won't. I've a few biscuits in my saddle bag and I want you to have them – that's all. It won't cost you. It's a present. I've had my supper and you haven't had yours. You can talk to me, son. I don't bite, you know. Look, son, I'll tell you what. I'll throw you over three biscuits today – that's all I've got – and then I'll come back tomorrow with some more. How's that?" As he talked he stood up and moved over to his horse and unbuckled his saddle bag. He took out the three meal biscuits he had left and held them up in the air. "Here you are, son. It's all I've got."

The boy stood up slowly, his line still lying in the water, his eyes never leaving the Dragoon's hand. He spoke softly, but with not a trace of supplication. "Don't throw them, mister," he said. "I'll come across."

"Meet you half-way, son," said the Dragoon, exhilarated that the child had spoken to him at last.

They met in mid-stream and the Dragoon looked down at the boy as he handed him the biscuits.

"Shall I come back tomorrow, son? Same time, same place? Will you be here, son?"

"Could be," said the boy, holding the biscuits tight in his hands and smelling them as if to confirm their reality. "Maybe I will," he said.

"What are you called, son? What do they call you at home?"

"Sean," said the boy, never for one moment taking his eyes from the biscuits. "I'm called Sean O'Brien."

Michael Morpurgo from *Twist of Gold*
(Mammoth)

Glossary
Dragoon: soldier in a cavalry unit

 Answer in sentences.

1   How did the Dragoon feel about being hated by Irish children? *(1 mark)*

2   Who had told the boy to have nothing to do with soldiers? *(1 mark)*

3   How could the Dragoon tell that the boy was starving and close to death?
     (2 marks)

4   The Dragoon was "exhilarated" when the boy spoke to him at last.

     a) What does "exhilarated" mean? *(1 mark)*
     b) What does this reaction tell us about the Dragoon? *(1 mark)*

5   Suggest words which could take the place of those underlined in the
     sentences below.

     a) The man sensed the boy's burning <u>enmity</u>. *(1 mark)*
     b) He had <u>encountered</u> it often enough before. *(1 mark)*
     c) The truth dawned on him in all its <u>clarity</u>. *(1 mark)*

6   What was the Dragoon's first name? *(0.5 mark)*

7   What was the boy's first name? *(0.5 mark)*

8   Explain in your own words the underlined parts of these sentences:

     a) It was a close, still evening and <u>the flies were down.</u> *(1 mark)*
     b) The boy <u>baited his hook.</u> *(1 mark)*
     **c) The Dragoon's horse stood with his legs in the cool of the water and
         <u>drank tidily.</u>** *(1 mark)*

9   What do you feel is especially significant in the boy and the Dragoon meeting
     mid-way across the river? *(1 mark)*

10   What does the boy's body language tell us about what he was feeling when the
     biscuits were given to him? (He held them tightly; he smelt them; he didn't take
     his eyes off them.) *(1 mark)*

UNIT 17

Learn to read or get lost

These pages come from a public information leaflet produced in Scotland.

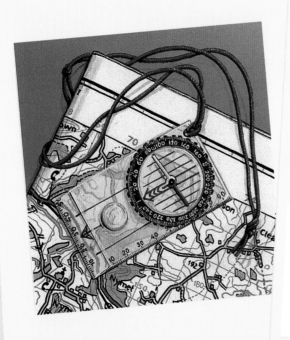

LEARN TO READ OR GET LOST

INTRODUCTION

Every year, tourists, walkers and climbers get into trouble in the Scottish hills due to errors in navigation. If you intend to go into the Scottish hills, even low ones, it is essential that you plan the walk using appropriate maps of the area. Those produced by Ordnance Survey are ideal.

Work out roughly how long the walk you have selected should take – this will depend on the fitness of the weakest member of your party and a variety of other factors:

- STEEPNESS OF THE GROUND – you may have to zig-zag your route for comfort.
- TERRAIN – walking is often harder than the map would suggest due to boulders, scree or boggy, vegetated ground.
- WEATHER – bad weather and poor visibility can dramatically affect estimated times.
- STREAMS – these can quickly become impassable in heavy rain.

PLAN AHEAD

If you are inexperienced and/or you do not know the area, seek local advice about the route.

Get instruction and learn how to use a map and your compass, starting in easy situations in good weather and practising until you are competent in poor weather. Before leaving your base, work out and keep a note of any bearings that you may require on the walk.

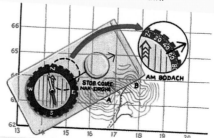

TAKING A COMPASS BEARING FROM THE MAP

Also, you should plan an alternative route in case conditions deteriorate or become worse than expected. Do not feel obliged to carry on, however – remember that often the safest option is to turn back early.

Always leave the route of your intended and alternative routes with a responsible person and make sure you contact him or her on your return.

ON THE HILL

When you are on the hills in good visibility, even when on paths, pay close attention to the map and make sure you are where you think you are and are going in the right direction. Do not wait until you are unsure of your position before using your map and compass – it could be too late!

IN POOR VISIBILITY

If mist closes in, use the compass to maintain your direction. Note ground features and estimate their position and distance from you and judge how long it will take you to reach them. Pay particular attention to the information given by the contour lines on the map.

Take extra care when leaving summits or where ridges meet. Gross errors are made here and when descending slopes in poor visibility – many parties become split up or lost in this phase of the walk.

WHEN LOST

If you become unsure of your position, either retrace your tracks to your last known position or, after working out roughly where you are and if the terrain is safe, head in the direction that will take you back on course.

If you get completely lost, stop or consider which is the safest direction to get off the hill or mountain. Use the compass to travel carefully in that direction until you recognise features and relocate yourself.

SETTING THE MAP WITH FEATURES ON THE GROUND.

KEY POINTS TO REMEMBER

1. Learn to use the compass before you need to use it for real.

2. Study the map and plan your route so that you know where you want to go and how long it should take.

3. Always set the map in relation to the ground.

4. Always have the map and compass handy during the walk.

5. Check your position at all times.

6. Leave a note of your intended route and time of return with a responsible person.

from leaflet *Learn to read or get lost*
(Scottish Mountain Safety Group)

 Answer in sentences.

1 What two things do you need to be able to read to avoid getting lost on the Scottish hills or mountains? *(2 marks)*

2 Why is it a good idea to plan two routes before you go walking or climbing? *(1 mark)*

3 Why should you always tell a responsible person where you are going? *(1 mark)*

4 Why is it so difficult to calculate in advance how long a walk will take in the Scottish hills and mountains? Give as many reasons as you can. *(4 marks)*

5 Which word in the first section ("Introduction") means "slippery stretches of rock fragments on steeply sloping ground"? *(1 mark)*

6 Why is it a good idea to seek local advice? *(1 mark)*

7 Why should you always study a map of the area carefully before you set off? *(1 mark)*

8 Why should you take a map with you when you go walking or climbing? *(2 marks)*

9 Why do you need to take a compass with you? *(1 mark)*

10 What are you advised to do if you get completely lost? *(1 mark)*

Meeting

*Willie and the other children with the Billeting Officer are evacuees.
They have been moved to the countryside away from the towns and cities
where their homes are, just as the Second World War is about to begin.*

"Yes," said Tom bluntly, on opening the front door. "What d'you want?"

A harassed middle-aged woman in a green coat and felt hat stood
on his step. He glanced at the armband on her sleeve. She gave him an
awkward smile.

"I'm the Billeting Officer for this area," she began.

"Oh yes, and what's that got to do wi' me?"

She flushed slightly. "Well, Mr, Mr ..."

"Oakley, Thomas Oakley."

"Ah, thank you, Mr Oakley." She paused and took a deep breath.
"Mr Oakley, with the declaration of war imminent ..."

Tom waved his hand. "I knows all that. Git to the point. What
d'you want?" He noticed a small boy at her side.

"It's him I've come about," she said. "I'm on my way to your village
hall with the others."

"What others?"

She stepped to one side. Behind the large iron gate which stood at
the end of the graveyard was a small group of children. Many of them
were filthy and very poorly clad. Only a handful had a blazer or coat.
They all looked bewildered and exhausted. One tiny dark-haired girl in
the front was hanging firmly on to a new teddy bear.

The woman touched the boy at her side and pushed him forward.

"There's no need to tell me," said Tom. "It's obligatory and it's for
the war effort."

"You are entitled to choose your child, I know," began the woman
apologetically.

Tom gave a snort.

"But," she continued, "his mother wants him to be with someone
who's religious or near a church. She was quite adamant. Said she
would only let him be evacuated if he was."

"Was what?" asked Tom impatiently.

"Near a church."

Tom took a second look at the child. ⇨

The boy was thin and sickly-looking, pale with limp sandy hair and dull grey eyes.

"His name's Willie," said the woman.

Willie, who had been staring at the ground, looked up. Round his neck, hanging from a piece of string, was a cardboard label. It read "William Beech".

Tom was well into his sixties, a healthy, robust, stockily-built man with a head of thick white hair. Although he was of average height, in Willie's eyes he was a towering giant with skin like coarse, wrinkled brown paper and a voice like thunder.

He glared at Willie. "You'd best come in," he said abruptly.

The woman gave a relieved smile. "Thank you so much," she said, and she backed quickly away and hurried down the tiny path towards the other children. Willie watched her go.

"Come on in," repeated Tom harshly. " I ent got all day."

Nervously, Willie followed him into a dark hallway. It took a few seconds for his eyes to adjust from the brilliant sunshine he had left to the comparative darkness of the cottage. He could just make out the shapes of a few coats hanging on some wooden pegs and two pairs of boots standing below.

"S'pose you'd best know where to put yer things," muttered Tom, looking up at the coat rack and then down at Willie. He scratched his head. "Bit 'igh fer you. I'd best put in a low peg."

He opened a door on his left and walked into the front room, leaving Willie in the hallway still clutching onto his brown carrier bag. Through the half-open door he could see a large black cooking range with a fire in it and an old threadbare armchair nearby. He shivered. Presently Tom came out with a pencil.

"You can put that ole bag down," he said gruffly. "You ent goin' no place else."

Willie did so and Tom handed him the pencil. He stared blankly up at him.

"Go on," said Tom. "I told you before. I ent got all day. Now make a mark so's I know where to put a peg, see." Willie made a faint dot on the wall beside the hem of one of the large coats. "Make a nice big 'un so's I can see it clear, like." Willie drew a small circle and filled it in. Tom leaned down and peered at it. "Neat little chap, ent you. Gimme yer mackintosh and I'll put it on top o' mine fer now."

With shaking fingers Willie undid his belt and buttons, peeled off the mackintosh and held it in his arms. Tom took it from him and hung it on top of his greatcoat. He walked back into the front room. "Come on," he said. Willie followed him in.

It was a small, comfortable room with two windows. The front one looked out on to the graveyard, the other to a little garden at the side. The large black range stood solidly in an alcove in the back wall, a thick dark pipe curving its way upward through the ceiling. Stretched out beneath the side window were a few shelves filled with books, old newspapers and odds and ends and by the front window stood a heavy wooden table and two chairs. The flagstoned floor was covered in a faded crimson, green and brown rug. Willie glanced at the armchair by the range and the objects that lay on top of the small wooden table beside it; a pipe, a book and a baccy jar.

"Pull that stool up by the fire and I'll give you somethin' to eat."

Willie made no movement. "Go on, sit down, boy," he repeated. "You got wax in your ears?"

Willie pulled a small wooden stool from a corner and sat down in front of the fire. He felt frightened and lonely.

Tom cooked two rashers of bacon and placed a slab of bread, with the fresh bacon dripping beside it, onto a plate.

"Eat that up," said Tom.

Willie dragged himself reluctantly from the warmth of the fire and sat at the table. "You can put yer own sugar in," Tom grunted.

Willie politely took a spoonful, dunked it into the large white mug of tea and stirred it. He bit into the bread but a large lump in his throat made swallowing difficult. He didn't feel at all hungry, but remembered apprehensively what his Mum had said about doing as he was told. He stared out at the graveyard. The sun shone brilliantly, yet he felt cold. He gazed at the few trees around the graves. Their leaves were all different colours,

pale greens, amber, yellow ...

"Ent you 'ungry?" asked Tom from his armchair.

Willie looked up startled. "Yes, mister," he whispered.

"Jest a slow chewer, that it?"

He nodded timidly and stared miserably at the plate. Bacon was a luxury. Only lodgers or visitors had bacon and here he was not eating it.

"Mebbe you can chew it more easy later." Tom beckoned him over to the stool. "Put another spoon of that sugar in, boy, and bring that tea over 'ere."

Willie did so and returned to the stool. He held the warm mug tightly in his icy hands and shivered. Tom leaned towards him.

"What you got in yer bag, then?"

"I dunno," mumbled Willie. "Mum packed it. She said I weren't to look in." One of his socks slid half-way down his leg, revealing a large multi-coloured bruise on his shin and a swollen red sore beside.

"That's a nasty ole thing," Tom said, pointing to it. "What give you that?" Willie paled and pulled the sock up quickly.

"Best drink that afore it gits cold," said Tom, sensing that the subject needed to be changed. Willie looked intently at the changing shapes of the flames in the fire and slowly drank the tea. It thundered in his throat in his attempt to swallow it quietly. Tom left the room briefly and within a few minutes returned.

"I gotta go out for a spell. Then I'll fix your room, see. Up there," and he pointed to the ceiling. "You ent afraid of heights, are you?" Willie shook his head. "That's good or you'd have had to sleep under the table." He bent and shovelled some fresh coke into the fire.

"'Ere's an ole scarf of mine," he muttered, and he threw a khaki object over Willie's knees. He noticed another bruise on the boy's thigh, but said nothing. "'Ave a wander round the graveyard. Don't be scared of the dead. Least they can't drop an ole bomb on yer head."

"No, mister," agreed Willie politely.

"And close the front door behind you, else Sammy'll be eatin' your bacon."

"Yes, mister."

Willie heard him slam the front door and listened to the sound of his footsteps gradually fading. He hugged himself tightly and rocked backwards and forwards on the stool.

"I must be good," he whispered urgently. "I must be good," and he rubbed a sore spot on his arm. He was such a bad boy, he knew that. Mum said she was kinder to him than most mothers. She only gave him soft beatings. He shuddered. He was dreading the moment when Mr Oakley would discover how wicked he was. He was stronger-looking than Mum.

Michelle Magorian from *Goodnight Mister Tom*
(Puffin)

Answer in sentences.

1   Why was the Billeting Officer "relieved" when Tom Oakley agreed to let Willie live with him? *(1 mark)*

2   Why was she wearing an armband? *(1 mark)*

3   Which word tells us that she was not finding her job of placing the children in foster homes an easy one? *(1 mark)*

4   What did she mean when she said that the declaration of war was "imminent"? *(1 mark)*

5   In what ways was Tom Oakley's appearance the very opposite of Willie's? *(2 marks)*

6   Why did Willie have so many bruises? *(1 mark)*

7   What clues are there in the passage that show Tom was really a kind man although he sounded fierce? *(2 marks)*

8   Why was Willie so desperately anxious to "be good"? *(1 mark)*

9   Write a paragraph on what you learn about Willie's background from this extract. *(3 marks)*

10 What is the meaning of the underlined words?

    a) "His mother wants him to be with someone who's religious or near a church. She was quite <u>adamant</u>." *(0.5 mark)*

    b) He didn't feel at all hungry, but remembered <u>apprehensively</u> what his Mum had said about doing as he was told. *(0.5 mark)*

    c) Bacon was a luxury. Only <u>lodgers</u> or visitors had bacon and here he was not eating it. *(0.5 mark)*

    d) One of his socks slid half-way down his leg, revealing a large <u>multi-coloured</u> bruise on his shin. *(0.5 mark)*

Homework's coming home

Pupils in Britain do less homework than in other countries. *John O'Leary* asks if they should do more.

Homework's coming home

Surveys show that British pupils between the ages of 7 and 12 do much less homework than their counterparts in France, Germany, Japan, China or the United States. An American market research company found that only 42 per cent of the British sample were set work on three or more evenings a week, compared with 90 per cent or more elsewhere.

By the age of 14, the average homework load in Britain has risen to six hours a week, although the variations between schools are immense. In Hungary, Holland, Poland, Israel, Italy and Japan, the average is more than eight hours.

A study by the National Foundation for Educational Research found that more than 40 per cent of 11-year-olds were never expected to take work home. In the following year, after transfer to secondary school, almost two thirds of pupils were doing less than Labour's recommended 90 minutes per night.

In many independent and grammar schools, however, as well as the more academic comprehensives, overload is the main concern. For every disgruntled parent who feels that their child is not being stretched, there is another worried about the pressure of projects and coursework. Conscientious girls, in particular, will toil late into the night.

At King Edward VI Handsworth School for Girls in Birmingham, one of the top state schools, the norm for 11- to 13-year-olds has been reduced from 90 minutes to an hour a night because of fears that other activities were suffering. Elspeth Insch, the Principal, said: "Cutting the time spent on homework does not mean we don't think it's important. I think it is vital to the learning process. But in our case the girls were doing too much."

Professor Michael Barber's report for the Department for Education and Employment conceded, like others before, that no link could be proved between hours of homework and improved examination results.

"At first I thought, this is horrible"

Name: Lucy Adams, 11
School: Bellview School, Essex (mixed comprehensive), Year 7
Homework: 9 hours/week
"My first reaction was 'yuk, this is horrible'. I wish we'd done some more homework at my primary school."

Janet Adams (mother)
"Her homework routine is disciplined: I am responsible for ensuring that she completes her tasks. One problem with switching the responsibility on to parents is that you are frightened of interfering in your child's homework. You are also apprehensive as to whether you will actually be able to answer their questions, especially if you aren't academic yourself."

"Digging in books can be fun"

Name: Emily Smith, 10
School: St Paul's C of E Primary, Halstead, Essex, Year 5
Homework: 2 hours/week
"Most of what I have to do is research – finding out the names of capital cities, that kind of thing. Our teacher likes to set us challenges for the next day.

It can be fun, digging around in books for information, asking Mum and Dad questions. My mum thinks that I should have more homework to do but I think what I do is about right – I do about two hours a week. Not everyone in my class agrees: one boy really hates doing homework and causes a terrible fuss whenever it is set. When I go to senior school I know I will have to do a lot more homework so it's good to start early."

Melanie Smith (mother)
"Emily is a very bright child but sometimes I feel that she is not pushed hard enough at school. She is given homework but it tends to be unstructured, revolving around research and finishing off what she has been doing during the day."

"For me homework is a fact of life"

Name: Daniel Wright, 13
School: The Boys School, Cambridge (private boarding),
Class North A, Year 9
Homework: 8 hours/week
"For me homework – prep as we call it – is a fact of life, it's something you have to do.

We have two prep sessions an evening and there is also a Saturday session. The sessions are structured, being overseen by a tutor or a sixth-former."

Paula Wright (mother)
"Before Daniel became a boarder he did a lot of homework as a matter of routine. I was horrified to read this week a report which suggested that 43 per cent of primary school pupils received no regular homework.
I always thought it was standard that all children did homework, but I am against any attempt to dictate how much they do. It's no good telling children that they should spend an hour on a piece of work, because what each child can produce in that time varies wildly."

"School is quite severe"

Name: Peter Miller, 14
School: Smithfield High (boys' comprehensive), Class 4A
Homework: 16 hours/week

"Sometimes it is a struggle to complete all the work, sometimes I forget that I have to hand something in and end up rushing it at the last minute. The school is quite severe to you if you don't do your homework. I have had a couple of detentions for not producing work on time."

Carol Miller (mother)

"Peter has such an active life that it can be a struggle getting him to dedicate enough time to his homework. He goes to Scouts, he is studying for his Duke of Edinburgh awards and plays the flute in several school bands. But what he really wants to do is work on the farm. He doesn't want to do his homework at all. As a result, I have to keep encouraging him to stick at it, especially at the end of term when he is tired. You are actively involved in homework through being required to sign your child's homework diary. If the diary isn't signed your son gets into trouble. If you feel that he is having difficulties with his work or is worried about something you are encouraged to write a note in the diary."

John O'Leary adapted from *The Times*, 20 January 1997 ▷

Answer in sentences.

1   Why has the Principal of King Edward VI Handsworth School for Girls reduced the amount of homework set to eleven- to thirteen-year-olds at her school? *(1 mark)*

2   Does Peter Miller at Smithfield High do more or less homework per week than the average British fourteen-year-old? Explain. *(1 mark)*

3   Out of the four pupils interviewed:
    a) **Who enjoys doing homework the most?** *(0.5 mark)*
    b) **Who enjoys doing it the least?** *(0.5 mark)*

4   True or false? Write out the statements that are true: *(3 marks)*
    a) **Most pupils in British primary schools do not have homework.**
    b) **Dutch fourteen-year-old pupils have more homework on average than British fourteen-year-olds.**
    c) **Girls are more likely than boys to spend hours and hours on their homework.**
    d) **Nobody has yet proved that doing homework helps you get better exam results.**
    e) **Teachers may expect homework to take a certain amount of time to do but some children will need more time and some less.**

5   Why does Lucy Adams wish she had been given more homework at primary school? *(1 mark)*

6   Why would Mrs Smith like her daughter to have more homework? *(1 mark)*

7   a) What does Daniel Wright mean when he says his homework sessions are overseen? *(1 mark)*
    b) Do you think this is a good idea? Give your reasons. *(1 mark)*

8   How do some schools involve parents in checking that homework is done? *(1 mark)*

9   In what way is Peter Miller's school "quite severe" when homework is not done? *(1 mark)*

10 Explain the meaning of these words as they are used in the main article:
    a) **counterparts** (paragraph one) *(0.5 mark)*
    b) **sample** (paragraph one) *(0.5 mark)*
    c) **disgruntled** (paragraph four) *(0.5 mark)*
    d) **conscientious** (paragraph four) *(0.5 mark)*
    e) **vital** (paragraph five) *(0.5 mark)*
    f) **conceded** (last paragraph) *(0.5 mark)*

Monsoon

The monsoon winds bring torrential rain to India every June and can bring cities there to a standstill. It is Hari's first year in Bombay. He has come from a small village to earn money to help his mother and sisters.

"The monsoon is coming!" shouted old Mr Panwallah, stepping back from the sea wall as a huge wave came crashing against it, throwing out a whiplash of spray at the crowd collected on the promenade to watch. "See, Hari, the monsoon is coming!"

Hari nodded, laughing as the spray drenched him. The crowd fled backwards as yet another wave came to break against the wall with a crash, and another. The whole sea was in turmoil, great black waves rearing out of it and storming towards the shore. There were no clouds in the sky yet, but the sea seemed to know they were on the way, and was rushing forwards and upwards to meet them.

Mr Panwallah had brought Hari to the Worli seaface to see the approach of the monsoon. He said he did this every year on a day in the first week of June. He had pulled down the shutters of his shop early, straightened the black cap on his head, asked Jagu to give Hari an evening off, and brought him here on the bus. He had also insisted on buying Hari a green coconut and a paper cone filled with puffed rice. Hari was shaking the cone into his hand and eating the puffed rice just like one of those lucky children brought here by their parents for an outing, enjoying themselves on the merry-go-rounds set up along the promenade and buying balloons and ice-creams and coconuts. It made him feel one of them, a child again – not a small, shrivelled adult keeping up with the other adults in a hard world. The roaring wind off the sea with its salty tang, the sharp sting of spray from the waves and the sight of the great ocean stretching out all the way to Africa made him feel lighter and happier than he could remember feeling for a long time. "Thank you, Mr Panwallah," he remembered to say. He did not know that evening how hard the monsoon made life for the people of Bombay.

On the tenth of June it came storming out of the sea and pouring onto the city just as Mr Panwallah had said it would. Like all the other citizens of Bombay, Hari stayed indoors and watched the rain like a great sheet being flung upon the city, and the water rising in the streets. ⬎

The street in front of the eating house became first a gutter – all the
rubbish of a year suddenly lifted up and carried away in a rush – and
then a river. The drains became blocked, the rising tide forced the water
up the big drain holes back into the streets, and they were flooded. Cars
broke down and stalled in knee-deep greasy water.

For a while the urchins in the city had a wonderful time out in the
rain, putting their shoulders to the cars and pushing them up to the
higher reaches and earning some coins from the drivers. Hari and the
two boys from the kitchen went out and made some pocket money, too,
and for the first time Hari saw his two fellow-cooks laughing as in
drenched shirts and shorts, with wet faces and streaming hair, they
demanded money from the drivers and heaved cars and taxis out of the
first patches of water-logging.

The city was washed clean not only of a year's dirt but also of the summer's heat, and the sudden dramatic drop in temperature gave everyone a lift: it was like a picnic, or a holiday. In fact it *was* a holiday for all the school children who could not get to school dry and therefore were not sent at all, and the office workers who could not get to work because buses and trains had stalled in the water that rose higher by the minute. "Soon we'll need boats!" the urchins shouted as they splashed through the flood.

But it was not really a holiday for Hari and the two boys in the kitchen. Coolies and hand-cart pullers who could not get any work done came to sit in the Sri Krishna Eating House and asked for tea and hot meals. Jagu called in the boys from the street to get down to work. They worked overtime, without any break. The coal and the wood had all gone damp and it was difficult to get a fire started. When they did, it did not burn but smouldered and smoked, getting into their eyes and throats and making them cough and rub at their eyes with grimy hands. The customers brought mud into the eating room which had to be cleaned up constantly with a rag and a pail that soon seemed filled with mud. Sometimes they were made to go out and fetch cigarettes and they were drenched and could not get dry but shivered miserably.

By evening Hari was more tired than he had ever been before, and it was still raining, pouring. He suddenly realised he would not be able to sleep in the park tonight – and perhaps not on any night during the monsoon. When Jagu put out the light and took out the key to lock up the place for the night, Hari knew he could not go out into the rain and there was nothing to do but stretch out on the bench in the suffocating room and try to sleep. Of course he could not. That night he felt like a prisoner on his first night in jail.

It rained day and night, week after week. Even when the rain slowed from a downpour to a drizzle and the flood receded, nothing dried out, everything remained damp and muddy and smelt. Every time Hari went out to empty the rubbish pail or to buy cigarettes for the customers, his shirt was soaked again and he spent the rest of the day with the wet cloth clinging to his body. He began to cough so badly that his chest hurt.

Mr Panwallah next door felt even worse and sniffed and coughed and wheezed without stopping. ⇨

One day he did not appear to pull the shutter up: he was sick. Now Hari had no escape at all from the kitchen and the eating house, since he could go neither to the watch shop nor to the park. Locked up day and night in the Sri Krishna Eating House, he began to feel like a prisoner condemned to live in a prison cell.

Anita Desai from *The Village by the Sea*
(Penguin)

Answer in sentences.

1 How can you tell from the passage that the monsoon comes regularly to India every year? *(1 mark)*

2 Explain the meaning of: "The city was washed clean not only of the year's dirt but also of the summer's heat". *(2 marks)*

3 How did Hari earn some extra pocket money on June 10th? *(1 mark)*

4 In what ways did the monsoon make life much more difficult for the boys working at the Sri Krishna Eating House? *(2 marks)*

5 Why was it particularly difficult for Hari to sleep at night during the monsoon? *(1 mark)*

6 What did Mr Panwallah do for a living? *(1 mark)*

7 In what ways was Mr Panwallah a good friend to Hari? *(3 marks)*

8 Explain in what sense Hari was "locked up night and day" in the Sri Krishna Eating House. *(1 mark)*

9 What is the meaning of these words in the passage?
   a) drenched (paragraph two) *(0.5 mark)*
   b) dramatic (paragraph six) *(0.5 mark)*
   c) stalled (paragraph six) *(0.5 mark)*
   d) receded (paragraph nine) *(0.5 mark)*

10 Which word in the passage means "tumult"? *(1 mark)*

Fiction: legend

The sword in the stone

The story of King Arthur is an ancient tale, set in a time when Britain was just a collection of separate kingdoms, and knights battled with one another for power. Many different versions of the story have been told. Many people believe that Camelot, where King Arthur lived, was located at Caerleon in South Wales.

This extract tells the story of how the young Arthur becomes King, at a huge meeting of knights in Canterbury.

"You're a couple of fine lads," the knight said as the two stood before him, panting and bright-eyed with the excitement and exercise. "I wouldn't choose between the two of you. My master will be pleased."

"What master do you mean, Father?" asked Arthur.

"I cannot name him to you yet," said Sir Ector, "but I think the day cannot be far away. Now, Kay: I have in mind to take you to the great meeting of knights that has been called in Canterbury. Do you think you're ready to take your place with the best in the land?"

"I think so, Father," said Kay seriously.

"And Arthur, will you ride with him as his squire?"

"Gladly, sir."

"Aye," said Ector. "I think the time is come." But neither Kay nor Arthur knew why their father's face grew thoughtful, with a hint of sadness in it.

Arthur had never seen so many knights, so many horses, so many swords and spears. There were so many tents on the plain surrounding the cathedral that a man could not walk round them all in half a day. Arthur knew because he and Kay had tried, and lost themselves more than once in the confusion of horses, beggars, pedlars, quarrelling squires, yelping dogs searching for scraps, great fires where whole oxen were roasted. Everywhere there was noise and colour – a bewildering rainbow of pennants, for knights and kings had come to Canterbury from all over Britain, from the far islands, and even from the lands across the great sea.

Arthur gazed in awe at men he had half thought existed only in stories and legends. There rode King Bors of Gaunes, shorter than Arthur had imagined him – so great warriors didn't have to be tall! – ⇨

but broad as an oak tree, his huge bass laugh ringing out as he passed with his young cousin, Lancelot, whose long fair hair streamed in the wind. And could he really be seeing King Lot of Orkney, Lot of the Thousand Battles? Arthur stared at the scarred face, the fierce eyes under lowered brows, looking neither to left or right as he rode between the lines of tents. His sword was not bright, as Arthur had imagined; it was stained and pitted, dents and spots along its whole length. Arthur thought about how those marks had been got, and for a moment he was glad that he had come to Canterbury as a squire and not a knight.

"Why does King Lot look so grimly, Father?" he asked Ector.

"It's a grim thing to be a warrior king," replied Ector. "See how men make way for him. Since Uther died, his arm has been the strongest, but he must know that one day as he gets older a stronger man will come. And that's a grim thought."

But Lot had particular reason to look grim that day. On that morning a great wonder had appeared in the cathedral court; a huge stone with an anvil embedded in it, and a sword plunged through the anvil into the rock beneath. On the stone was an inscription: *THE MAN WHO DRAWS THIS SWORD SHALL BE THE RIGHTFUL KING OF BRITAIN*. Lot had come to the court to find a crowd of knights and lesser kings, each of them taking turns as they tried in vain to pull the sword from the anvil, watched by the Archbishop of

Canterbury and the wizard Merlin, who had come this day for reasons of his own, though no one had seen him since Uther Pendragon's death. The knights had given way when Lot came. He had stood astride the stone, tugged with his great strength, and the sword had not moved. "The thing is impossible," he said, and believed it too. But Merlin had smiled and said, "The thing is impossible for any but the true-born King of England." Bors had laughed. Bors of Gaunes laughed at him! But the wizard had more to say:

"The man has not yet come to heal the wounds of this sad land. But he is coming. I did not journey out of the West this winter for nothing. Be sure of this, all of you; a greater man than any of you is coming. Now pray with me in the Abbey as we await him."

Lot had turned his back on Merlin and headed for his tent; he had little time for wizards and their prophecies. But rivals had seen him fail, and a warrior king should never be seen to fail. That was why Lot looked so grim.

Next morning, bustling along in the throng of knights as they neared the Abbey for the service of blessing, Sir Ector was not his usual calm self. Since daybreak he had been showering poor Kay with instructions, warnings and good advice until the lad didn't know which way to turn. It was not surprising that as they turned into the Cathedral court, he pulled his horse up and gasped in horror: "My sword! I left it in our tent!" ▷

The knights were thronging into the abbey; there was clearly no time for Kay to ride back and fetch it. But Arthur cried, "Kay, I know where I've seen an old sword nearby! It'll serve you well enough till we can send for your own!" And he was away before Sir Ector could call him back.

Arthur ran into the little courtyard where he'd glimpsed the sword as they passed. The courtyard was deserted, damp and grey; the winter sun had not yet reached it. But the sword was there, its hilt sticking invitingly up out of some old block, like a woodcutter's axe.

Arthur leapt lightly up on to the stone and clasped the handle; the old sword slid out easily with a gentle whisper like the rustle of silk.

He turned to see Ector and Kay in the courtyard, standing stock-still and staring at him in amazement.

"What is it?" said Arthur. "Have I done wrong?"

"Put the sword back, Arthur," said Sir Ector in a strange new voice. Puzzled and apprehensive, Arthur did as he was told.

"Draw it out, Kay."

Kay struggled till the veins stood out on his forehead, but he could not move the sword an inch.

"Draw it again, Arthur."

And again the sword slipped whispering out of the stone. Arthur saw that Ector and Kay were kneeling on the damp cobbles.

"Father?" he said. "What are you doing? Why do you kneel to me?"

"Because I know from this," the old knight said slowly, "that you are the true-born king of this land."

"But why me? Why not my brother?"

"Kay is not your brother, my lord, nor I your father."

Arthur stared at him in astonishment as he went on: "Merlin brought you to me as a baby. He is the master I spoke of. Merlin awaits you in the Abbey, with all the knights and barons. They are waiting to see their king."

Andrew Davies from *The Legend of King Arthur*
(*Armada*)

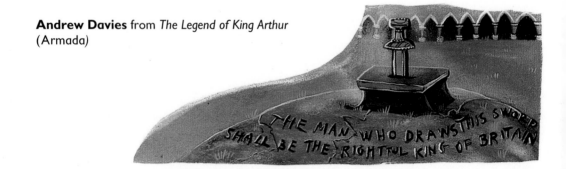

THE MAN WHO DRAWS THIS SWORD SHALL BE THE RIGHTFUL KING OF BRITAIN

1   What did Sir Ector mean when he asked Kay, "Do you think you're ready to take your place with the best in the land?"? *(1 mark)*

2   Why was there a "hint of sadness" on Sir Ector's face when the decision was made to go to Canterbury? *(1 mark)*

3   Sir Ector's old-fashioned style of speech is meant to reflect the ancient time in which he lived. Rewrite in up-to-date everyday English these speeches:
    a) "I cannot name him to you yet, but I think the day cannot be far away." *(1 mark)*
    b) "I have in mind to take you to Canterbury." *(1 mark)*
    c) "Aye, I think the time is come." *(1 mark)*

4   Why did the knights "give way" when King Lot of Orkney approached the sword in the stone? *(1 mark)*

5   "Since daybreak he had been showering poor Kay with instructions, warnings and good advice until the lad didn't know which way to turn." Explain why the word "showering" is a good word to use here. *(1 mark)*

6   Why did Sir Ector tell Arthur to put the sword back? *(1 mark)*
    a) Arthur should not have taken it out of the stone.
    b) Kay didn't want to use a shabby old sword.
    c) Sir Ector wanted to double-check what had happened.
    d) Sir Ector would have preferred Kay to fetch his own sword.

7   What made Arthur glad just "for a moment" that he had come to Canterbury as a squire and not as a knight? Explain. *(2 marks)*

8   We hear eventually who Sir Ector's "master" was. Name him. *(1 mark)*

9   The sword in the stone is described twice in the passage:
    i) ... a huge stone with an anvil embedded in it, and a sword plunged through the anvil into the rock beneath.
    ii) The sword was there, its hilt sticking invitingly up out of some old block, like a woodcutter's axe.
    You would think that two different swords and stones were being described!
    a) How does the sword seem quite different in the second description? *(1 mark)*
    b) How does the stone seem quite different in the second description? *(1 mark)*
    c) Why has the author done this deliberately? *(1 mark)*

10 "The old sword slid out easily with a gentle whisper like the rustle of silk." What makes this a good description? *(1 mark)*

UNIT 22

Mid-term break

While Seamus Heaney was away at boarding school, his young brother was killed in a road accident. In "Mid-term break", he writes about his vivid recollections of the day before the funeral.

I sat all morning in the college sick bay
Counting bells knelling classes to a close.
At two o'clock our neighbours drove me home.

In the porch I met my father crying –
He had always taken funerals in his stride –
And Big Jim Evans saying it was a hard blow.

The baby cooed and laughed and rocked the pram
When I came in, and I was embarrassed
By old men standing up to shake my hand

And tell me they were "sorry for my trouble";
Whispers informed strangers I was the eldest,
Away at school, as my mother held my hand

In hers and coughed out angry tearless sighs.
At ten o'clock the ambulance arrived
With the corpse, stanched and bandaged by the nurses.

Next morning I went up into the room. Snowdrops
And candles soothed the bedside; I saw him
For the first time in six weeks. Paler now,

Wearing a poppy bruise on his left temple,
He lay in the four foot box as in his cot.
No gaudy scars, the bumper knocked him clear.

A four foot box, a foot for every year.

Seamus Heaney from *The Puffin Book of Twentieth-Century Children's Verse*, ed. Brian Patten (Penguin)

![key icon] Read the poem carefully and answer these questions as fully as you can.

1   Why do you think his teachers decided that it was best for Seamus Heaney to stay in the sick bay that morning? *(1 mark)*

2   What does "close" mean in the first verse? *(1 mark)*

3   Why was Seamus Heaney embarrassed when his hand was shaken? *(2 marks)*

4   What does "stanched" (sometimes spelt "staunched") mean in verse five? *(1 mark)*

5   In what ways could candles and snowdrops "soothe" a bedside? *(2 marks)*

6   In what ways did the bruise on the little boy's forehead resemble a poppy? *(2 marks)*

7   What is the meaning of "gaudy" as it is used in the seventh verse? *(1 mark)*

8   List all the sounds from this day in his childhood that Seamus Heaney remembers vividly. *(2 marks)*

9   What time of year was it? How can you tell? *(1 mark)*

10 What makes the last line of this poem so moving? Find as many reasons as you can to explain why we are left feeling so sad. *(2 marks)*

23 Moon landing

She dreamed.

And the ship-voice called her.

"Wake up, Bethkahn!"

She opened her eyes. Light in the cryogenic chamber was dim blue and when she turned her head she could see through the transparent dome that covered her … curved silver walls and empty sleeping berths, a doorway leading into loneliness. She was the only one alive on a dead uncharted world and she could not bear it. The ship knew that and should not have woken her.

"What do you want?" she asked angrily.

The ship-voice hesitated before replying.

Then it told her.

"We are no longer alone here, mistress."

Bethkahn lay unmoving, not daring to believe, yet believing anyway in spite of herself. The ship would not lie to her. Rondahl had returned … Mahna had returned … the whole crew had returned. Elation filled her and all she had suffered seemed silly now that it was over. She wanted to leap from her berth, laugh and sing, rush wild through the blue-silver spaces to greet them. But she had been trained at the Galactic Academy and was no longer a child. She was a junior technician aboard an Explorer Class Starship and Rondahl would expect her to behave as one. But joy and relief spilled over in tears and she grinned stupidly, cried stupidly, not caring that the ship was watching her.

The ship had seen emotion before. At first she had had to tell it how she felt and why. But then it had learned to recognise cause and effect and although it could never share her feelings it seemed to understand. Through fear and panic, desperation and despair, it had done its best to comfort her. Now, seeing tears and smiles, its voice stayed silent, allowed her some moments to herself.

"How long have I been sleeping?" she asked it.

"Ten thousand orbital years," it replied.

She could not take it in. Ten thousand years was too long to imagine. Time in the cryogenic chamber had been suspended with her life, centuries compressed into seconds. It was as if she had slept and woken a moment later exactly as she was, untouched by age or experience. She laughed with the sheer joy of it and her thoughts turned back to the beginning.

A faulty stabiliser, Rondahl had said, as the ship spun sickeningly through pulsing dimensions of time and space. And spinning still it had slowed to sub-light speed, emerged among unknown suns in a remote arm of a spiral galaxy. They had landed on the attendant moon of an unknown planet to make repairs. To Rondahl it had seemed a bonus, that turquoise blue world turning in the black sky over them. Jewel-bright and beautiful it was waiting to be explored. The whole crew had gone there and Bethkahn had watched them leave ... a fleet of tiny survey craft, their wings catching the light, speeding over the crater rim to vanish among the stars. And she, being the junior technician, remained behind. She had to mend the stabiliser, Rondahl had said.

At first she had not really minded. Perhaps she had even been glad. Fresh from the Academy, an inexperienced girl on her initiation flight, it had not been easy. Mahna had been kind to her but Rondahl had ⇨

seen her as a nuisance, and the senior technicians had given her all the boring routine jobs to do. Adjusting the stabiliser was just one more. She had to remove the wall panel and crawl on her stomach through the flight control conduits.

The ship-voice had guided her. Usually it spoke only to Rondahl and Mahna who were in charge of it, but with Bethkahn alone on board she became its mistress. It had been a wonderful, awesome experience having the whole vast starship working for her and responding to her presence. It had given her a feeling of freedom and power and she had revelled in her solitude. She could command it to speak or be silent. She could draw on the knowledge contained in its computerised mind. There was a fault, it said, in number three stabiliser. Bethkahn found it blown, two metal blades sheered off under pressure and the whole stabilising unit needing to be replaced. But when she checked the storeroom she discovered they had run out of spares. She could have made a laser-weld but the power packs were all on empty. It was then Bethkahn realised they were in trouble.

"What shall I do?" she had asked the ship. "We can't take off without a stabiliser!"

"That's Rondahl's problem," it informed her. "You must leave it for him. He took the risk and I told him repeatedly I was due for an overhaul, and advised him to return to base. A ship knows best about itself but he paid me no heed. There's nothing you can do, Bethkahn."

So Bethkahn had learned that Rondahl the shipmaster was not perfect, and she waited nervously for his return. Suddenly time had assumed a meaning. She grew aware of its passing and needed to measure it. But the ship had nothing to go by. Parsecs and megaparsecs could not apply. They had to work it out by planetary motion, the moon and its world revolving around the nearby star. They had counted in moondays ... one ... two ... three ... eye-blinks in eternity. But Bethkahn, trapped in one space-time dimension, experienced its slowness. Solitude changed to loneliness and although the ship-voice kept her company it was not the same as having the crew around. Rooms and corridors oppressed her with their silences. She missed Mahna's laughter and Rondahl's frown. But down on the planet's surface they were absorbed in their survey and did not notice time. Bethkahn waited and waited. Half of one orbital year was nothing, the ship-voice had said.

Eventually she tried the transmitter but no one answered her. Lost on that blue bright world beneath its swirling atmosphere, she supposed they did not hear. She despatched the last long-range scanner. But the survey craft were hidden by drifts of white cloud and the life-traces of the crew were indistinguishable among millions of other life-traces. The planet teemed with primordial existences and neither Bethkahn nor the ship could identify the ones they knew. And when the probe burned up during a volcanic eruption her anxiety turned to panic.

The planet was geologically unstable and Rondahl might never return. Bethkahn might be trapped forever in a crippled starship far from the main flight paths. She would not listen to the ship-voice trying to calm her. She transmitted a general distress call across the galaxy, transmitted and transmitted until the delicate circuitry fused and was useless. Then she could do nothing else but wait ... through moondays blinding white and long airless nights, years turning to decades. How long her messages would take to reach the starbases only the ship could compute, but it would be thousands of years, it had said, before help would arrive. And then who would hear her? Her voice crying through a dead transmitter? Or see the starship buried in moondust under a millennium of time?

For her mistake Bethkahn had blamed the ship. She had screamed in her isolation and despair, beat with clenched fists on its cold curved walls, hating everything it was ... an unfeeling machine, a prison of white light, a useless metal artefact that could do nothing to help. Through years of madness she had gone outside and searched the moon's barren surface, looking for someone who would love her, arms that would hold her, another living being to comfort her and care. But nothing lived on its pock-marked surface. Nothing moved among its mountains and craters and oceans of dust.

The ship was all that remained for Bethkahn, her only sanctuary, her only friend.

Louise Lawrence from *Moonwind*
(Bodley Head) ⇨

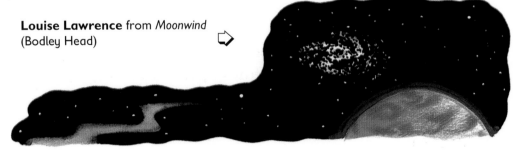

Answer in sentences.

1. Why was it necessary for the ship-voice to wake Bethkahn from her long sleep? *(1 mark)*

2. What is "cryogenics"? (A dictionary will help you.) *(1 mark)*

3. Explain why Bethkahn had not grown any older while she was in the cryogenic chamber (even though she had been in it for ten thousand years!). *(1 mark)*

4. Why is the name "Galactic Academy" a good name for the college Bethkahn attended? *(1 mark)*

5. What is the meaning of an "initiation flight"? *(1 mark)*

6. Explain how studying "cause and effect" taught the ship to understand Bethkahn's feelings. *(2 marks)*

7. Explain the difference between:
   a) fear and panic *(1 mark)*
   b) desperation and despair *(1 mark)*

8. Why had the rest of the crew left the starship? *(1 mark)*

9. Why was it Bethkahn who had to stay behind to mend the stabiliser? *(1 mark)*

10. Why was it vital to mend the stabiliser? *(1 mark)*

11. Why did Bethkahn find the waiting so difficult? *(1 mark)*

12. At the end of the extract, the ship is described as "her only friend".
    Explain how this contrasts with Bethkahn's earlier feelings about the ship. *(2 marks)*

Safety threatens to dampen fun of the fair

A Health and Safety Executive report into the safety of fairground rides which was classed last year as 'urgent' will come too late to make a difference this holiday season.

As thousands of children are already more than two weeks into the school holidays, and leisure parks and fairgrounds get busier, the HSE has been criticised for delaying a report which may have made fairgrounds a safer place.

Denise Kitchener, chief executive of the Association of Personal Injury Lawyers (APIL), said the report, which should have been released earlier in the year, will have little or no impact on fairground safety this summer.
"We understand the release of the report is imminent but it should have come much sooner," she said. "The HSE first started looking at this on an urgent basis last July. One year on, and we've already had one well-publicised death and no report from the HSE.

"What the industry needs is a complete overhaul of safety standards and tougher measures to make sure those standards don't slip. Five people died last year on fairground rides — we are concerned that unless urgent action is taken to shake up the industry we will see more serious accidents and deaths."

APIL believes current guidelines in place for fairground operators, organisers, ride owners and inspectors are not strict enough to ensure a high standard of safety.

The HSE admits in its fairground safety review that "events regarding examinations of fairground rides, particularly with respect to the competence and diligence of third-party examiners, have raised questions about the adequacy and application of the current regime."

"The HSE needs to clamp down on the way the fairground industry is regulated and it needs to act now," said Denise. "It is not compulsory for people to obtain the guidelines so how can we be certain that proper safety measures are in place?

"We just hope that when the report is issued it is detailed and strict enough to protect people from being thrown from rides because of loose

safety bars, or from other faults that can cost
lives. Sadly, it is already too late to make a
difference this season, but how many more tragic
and unnecessary deaths will we see before something
is done?"

Press release
Association of Personal Injury Lawyers (APIL)
August 2001

 Answer in sentences.

1   How many people died in fairground accidents in 2000? *(1 mark)*

2   The release of the HSE report is said to be 'imminent'. What does imminent mean? *(1 mark)*

3   Why does APIL claim in this press release that the report when it comes will have 'little or no impact' in 2001? *(1 mark)*

4   What is the response of the HSE to the criticism that fairground inspectors have not been doing a very good job? *(2 marks)*

5   Why are the HSE involved in what happens in fairgrounds? *((1 mark)*

6   Give one example from the passage of how poor maintenance of fairground equipment might cause a death. *(1 mark)*

7   What does APIL think of the present standards of fairground safety? *(2 marks)*

8   List three ways in which APIL thinks the present situation can be improved. *(3 marks)*

9   Why do you think APIL have issued this press release? *(1 mark)*

10   Look again at the title of the passage. In what way might safety 'dampen' the fun of the fair? *(2 marks)*

UNIT 25

Page from a dictionary of architecture

Greek orders

The ancient Greeks built important public buildings with an eye to harmony, proportion and balance. There were three principal orders (or styles): Doric, Ionic and Corinthian. The rules governing these applied to all parts of the building and especially to the supporting columns and entablatures. Columns consist of capital, shaft and (sometimes) a base and are surmounted by the entablature consisting of cornice, frieze and architrave.

The three orders are readily identified.

Doric	Ionic	Corinthian
column with fluted shaft, no base and a plain capital; entablature with a decorated frieze	column with fluted shaft, base and a capital with volutes; entablature with a plain frieze	column with a plain shaft, base, and a capital richly decorated with acanthus leaves; entablature with plain frieze

column	**capital, shaft, and (sometimes) base**
capital	the upper part of the column between the shaft and the architrave
fluting	having shallow vertical grooves
shaft	the part of the column below the capital (and above the base if there is one)
volutes	spiral scrolls looking like ram's horns
entablature	**architrave, frieze, and cornice**
architrave	the lowest band of the entablature
cornice	the upper band of the entablature
frieze	the middle band of the entablature

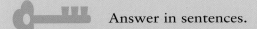 Answer in sentences.

1 What is the meaning of "principal" in "three principal orders"? *(1 mark)*

2 Explain how you would recognise a Corinthian column simply by looking at its capital. *(1 mark)*

3 The three orders are not listed alphabetically. Can you suggest what order they are in? *(2 marks)*

4 Which of the orders has a decorated frieze? *(1 mark)*

5 Name the six parts of the entablature and column in descending order from the top to the bottom. *(3 marks)*

6 Describe the decoration on an Ionic capital. *(1 mark)*

7 Which order has a plain shaft? *(1 mark)*

8 Explain what is meant by a fluted shaft. *(1 mark)*

9 What does 'vertical' mean? *(1 mark)*

10 Arrange these architectural terms in alphabetical order: pediment, plinth, parapet, purlin, pillar, pilaster. *(3 marks)*

UNIT 26

"Tarantella" and "Piano"

Tarantella

Do you remember an Inn,
Miranda?
Do you remember an Inn?

And the tedding and the spreading
Of the straw for a bedding,
And the fleas that tease in the High Pyrenees,
And the wine that tasted of the tar?
And the cheers and the jeers of the young muleteers
(Under the vine of the dark verandah)?
Do you remember an Inn, Miranda?
Do you remember an Inn?
And the cheers and the jeers of the young muleteers
Who hadn't got a penny,
And who weren't paying any,
And the hammer at the doors and the Din?
And the Hip! Hop! Hap!
Of the clap
Of the hands to the twirl and the swirl
Of the girl gone chancing,
Glancing,
Dancing,
Backing and advancing,
Snapping of a clapper to the spin
Out and in –
And the Ting, Tong, Tang of the guitar!
Do you remember an Inn,
Miranda?
Do you remember an Inn?

Hilaire Belloc from *The Rattlebag* eds. *Seamus Heaney and Ted Hughes* (Faber and Faber)

102

Piano

Softly, in the dusk, a woman is singing to me;
Taking me back down the vista of years, till I see
A child sitting under the piano, in the boom of the tingling strings
And pressing the small, poised feet of a mother who smiles as she sings.

In spite of myself, the insidious mastery of song
Betrays me back, till the heart of me weeps to belong
To the old Sunday evenings at home, with winter outside
And hymns in the cosy parlour, the tinkling piano our guide.

So now it is vain for the singer to burst into clamour
With the great black piano appassionato. The glamour
Of childish days is upon me, my manhood is cast
Down in the flood of remembrance. I weep like a child for the past.

D. H. Lawrence from *Touchstones 5 eds. Michael and Peter Benton* (Hodder and Stoughton)

 Answer in complete sentences.

1   "Both poets are remembering events in their past." Is this true? Explain. *(2 marks)*

2   What clues are there in "Tarantella" that the inn was in Spain? *(1 mark)*

3   List six different sounds that Belloc remembers hearing that evening. *(2 marks)*

4   We are almost dancing ourselves as we read the description of the girl dancing the tarantella. Why is this? *(2 marks)*

5   What has triggered D. H. Lawrence's memories of his childhood? *(1 mark)*

6   Why are his mother's feet "poised"? *(2 marks)*

7   Describe the differences between the two pianos in D. H. Lawrence's poem. *(2 marks)*

8   Why is D. H. Lawrence so sad at the end of his poem? *(1 mark)*

9   Which poem did you like best? Give your reasons. *(2 marks)*

Be wise on the net

INFORMATION FOR PARENTS AND GUARDIANS TO HELP CHILDREN STAY SAFE ON THE INTERNET

The Internet offers a wide range of learning and recreational opportunities for children. It provides opportunities to chat, email friends and research information across the globe. It is widely used in schools and homes as a learning tool and its educational benefits are increasingly appreciated by parents and teachers.

However!

The Internet is not controlled by any organisation and therefore there are risks involved with its use. It is understandable that every parent or guardian has concerns about these risks especially when most children appear to be either confident users or enthusiastic explorers. Many parents openly admit that they are not as comfortable with using the Internet as their children, but are keen to understand how they can actively play a role in the protection of their children while they are online.

Encourage your child to:

1 ▶ Store/bookmark the websites they visit in the favourites folder. Ideally these websites will have been previewed and approved by you.
2 ▶ Only use chat rooms that are 'age appropriate'. They should talk to you about the people they meet in chat rooms and should always stay in the public area of a chat room.
3 ▶ Avoid giving out any personal details such as name, phone number, address, school name or photo.
4 ▶ Never arrange or attend a face-to-face meeting with an online friend without the consent or presence of you or an adult you trust.
5 ▶ Report to you any invitations to meet online friends, pornography or anything that is upsetting.

from a leaflet 'Be Wise on the Net', published by NCTE (National Centre for Technology in Education)

True or false? Ten of the statements below are true. Find them and write them out carefully. *(15 marks: 1.5 marks for each statement correctly identified)*

1 Only foolish people think that children can be harmed by using the Internet.

2 Children should be warned never to meet an online friend face-to-face without discussing it first with a responsible adult.

3 Adults should not interfere with what their children do online.

4 Children should be discouraged from emailing their friends.

5 Children who come across anything disgusting or upsetting online should tell their parent or guardian.

6 The NCTE would like to ban computers in schools.

7 It is important never to reveal personal details to anyone online.

8 The Internet is not really suitable for adults.

9 There should always be a responsible adult sitting beside a child visiting a chat room.

10 This leaflet has been written to help parents and guardians keep their children safe online.

11 The Internet offers many benefits.

12 The Internet is completely safe.

13 Children are generally more confident about using computers than their parents.

14 "Age appropriate" means suitable for the age of the user.

15 Used sensibly, the Internet is a valuable educational tool.

16 Emailing friends is dangerous.

17 Parents and guardians can help to protect their children by taking an interest in the websites they visit.

18 Some chat rooms are not suitable for children.

All about tropical forests

Tropical forests grow near the **equator** in South America, Africa and Asia. There are also small areas of tropical forests in Australia, New Zealand and the Caribbean.

Climate

Tropical forests grow in areas where the **climate** is hot and wet. Temperatures are usually between 20°C and 28°C. It rains almost every day and there are usually thunderstorms in the afternoons.

Plant life

There are usually four layers of plants, all fighting to get to the light.

1 The **forest floor** is the lowest layer. It gets little sunlight so it is quite dark and gloomy. The floor is covered with mosses, **fungi**, ferns and rotten leaves.
2 The **understorey** is the next layer. Small trees, such as palms and young trees, sprout up in the gaps on the forest floor.
3 The **canopy** above the understorey is a mass of treetops that form a roof over the forest floor and trap warm air and most of the water from the rain.
4 The **emergent layer** is the highest layer. A few very tall trees have their tops here.

Animal life

On the forest floor you can see animals such as coatis, capybaras, jaguars and 'cock of the rock'. Coatis have long snouts for searching out grubs and insects. Jaguars are the largest cats in the tropical forest and 'cock of the rock' is a brightly coloured bird, which eats insects and berries.

The understorey is home to cats called ocelots and margays and also to lizards, anteaters, fruit bats and tarantulas. Tarantula spiders can grow to 26 cm (10 in) across. They eat other spiders, insects, frogs, small lizards and even birds.

The canopy is full of life. Creatures such as toucans, sloths, parrots, tamanduas, capuchin and woolly monkeys, snakes and macaws live here. The three-toed sloth hangs upside down on the branches of trees, using its powerful claws as hooks.

The emergent layer is home to spider and howler monkeys, opossums, the harpy eagle, hummingbirds and iguanas. Howler monkeys are the noisiest animals in the tropical forest.

http://www.heinemannexplore.com

 Answer in sentences.

1   Tropical forests grow principally in South America, Africa, and Asia. Where else can small areas be found? *(1 mark)*

2   Tropical forests flourish in hot, wet climates.
a) how hot? *(0.5 mark)*
b) how wet? *(0.5 mark)*

3   If you walked through a rainforest, you would find that it was very dark, even in the middle of the day. Why is this? *(2 marks)*

4   What grows on the lowest level of a rainforest? *(1 mark)*

5   What is meant by 'canopy' in the passage? *(1 mark)*

6   Do any trees grow higher than the level of the canopy? *(1 mark)*

7   a) What does the 'cock of the rock' feed on? *(0.5 mark)*
b) At what level in the forest is it found? *(0.5 mark)*

8   Which animal in the forest makes the most noise? *(1 mark)*

9   Are any animals found above the canopy level? *(1 mark)*

10   Why do coatis need their long snouts when searching for food? *(1 mark)*

11   Why don't we have rainforests in the British Isles? *(2 marks)*

12   'Fungi' grow on the forest floor. This is a plural noun. What is the singular of 'fungi'? *(1 mark)*

13   If you were reading this on-screen at your computer, what would happen if you clicked the glossary button? *(1 mark)*

UNIT 29

Council tax

How council tax is calculated

The amount of council tax that householders pay varies according to the valuation category of their house. This will have been decided by the Valuation Office. The categories are referred to as bands.

The following table shows how much Barsetshire County Council charged householders in each band in 2005.

Value of House as at 01.04.91	Council Tax Band	Tax due 2005	With 50% discount	With 25% discount
Under £40,000	A	£600.24	£300.12	£450.18
£40,000 - £52,000	B	£700.28	£350.14	£525.21
£52,001 - £68,000	C	£800.32	£400.16	£600.24
£68,001 - £88,000	D	£900.36	£450.18	£675.27
£88,001 - £120,000	E	£1,100.44	£550.22	£825.33
£120,001 - £160,000	F	£1,300.52	£650.26	£975.39
£160,001 - £320,000	G	£1,500.60	£750.30	£1,125.45
Over £320,000	H	£1,800.72	£900.36	£1,350.54

In addition, final council tax bills will include charges from the District Council, and possibly the Town or Parish Council.

Discounts

- Anyone living alone is entitled to a 25% discount.
- Owners of unoccupied property are entitled to a 50% discount.
- Those on low incomes may qualify for council tax benefit. The amount will depend on circumstances and the band the property has been put in by the Valuation Office.

How Barsetshire County Council spent the council tax in 2004

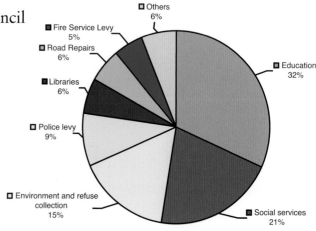

 Answer in sentences.

1   What are council tax 'bands'? *(1.5 marks)*

2   According to the spreadsheet, in which year did the Valuation Office value the houses? *(1.5 marks)*

3   What is a discount? *(1.5 marks)*

4   If you live in Barsetshire and your house is in Council Band H, how much council tax did you have to pay Barsetshire County Council in 2005? *(1.5 marks)*

5   Mr Green lives alone. What reduction in his council tax can he claim? *(1.5 marks)*

6   Mr and Mrs Duffy thought their final council tax in 2005 would be £600.24 but they had to pay £740.52. Their house is in Band A. What had they forgotten? *(1.5 marks)*

7   What proportion of their income from council tax did Barsetshire County Council have to pay to the Fire Service and the Police Authority in 2004? *(1.5 marks)*

8   What did Barsetshire County Council spend most of their income on in 2004? *(1.5 marks)*

9   The County Council improved 16 recycling centres and opened 9 new ones in 2005. What category will this come under in their pie chart of how the 2005 council tax was spent? *(1.5 marks)*

10   The County Council spent £120 million in 2004 on care for the elderly, the disabled, and children at risk. Where does this appear on the 2004 pie chart? *(1.5 marks)*

UNIT 30

The Wizard of Oz

Act 1: A farmyard with a fence and stile
(Uncle Henry is whistling to himself as he sharpens a scythe. Dorothy climbs over the stile and runs across to him.)

Dorothy	Hello, Uncle Henry.
Uncle Henry	Hello, Dorothy. What have you been up to today?
Dorothy	Oh, all sorts of things. We picked flowers in the wood and paddled in the stream, and we've walked miles.
Uncle Henry	Who have you been with?
Dorothy	Oh, just Toto. *(She takes her pet mouse from her pinafore pocket.)* I expect he's hungry. I'll have to get him some cheese. *(She strokes him.)* Isn't it peculiar, Uncle Henry? He understands everything I say.
Uncle Henry	I wish my animals understood what I said to them; it would save me a lot of time.
Dorothy	Perhaps they would if you talked to them as much as I talk to Toto.
Uncle Henry	You'd best not let him out of your sight. There's been an old ginger cat as big as a lion hanging about outside.
Dorothy	Oh! Uncle Henry! You don't mean it?
Uncle Henry	*(Chuckling)* No, he's quite safe.
Aunt Em	*(As she comes in.)* Henry! Have you put the animals away for the night? It looks like a storm brewing.
Dorothy	Toto doesn't like storms. Do you?
Uncle Henry	Nor do I. And I've seen my share. There have been some terrible storms not far away from here.
Aunt Em	Do you remember that great storm? The sky was just like this. It was long before you came to live with us, child. When we first came here.
Uncle Henry	It was more than just a storm; it was a cyclone.
Dorothy	A cyclone?
Uncle Henry	A mighty whirlwind that destroyed everything in its path; so powerful that it snapped great trees like twigs. That's why we made a cellar when we built this house – so that there would be somewhere to hide if another cyclone ever came.
Dorothy	Can a wind really be as strong as that?
Aunt Em	Child, there have been storms in these parts which lifted houses into the air and dropped them miles away.
Dorothy	How terrible! *(Changing the subject.)* Uncle Henry, can I help you when I come back from school tomorrow?
Uncle Henry	All right, I need somebody to lend a hand with the fence by the barn. And there's something else you can do. You can help me make a scarecrow.

Dorothy	A scarecrow! I'd love that.
Aunt Em	Henry! Hurry. I don't like the look of that sky.
Uncle Henry	I'll see to the animals now. *(He starts to go and Dorothy goes with him.)*
Aunt Em	*(Calling after them.)* You'd better hurry. It's getting dark. *(Aunt Em goes off. The sky gets darker. There is a crash of thunder and the sound of rushing wind. Aunt Em hurries back, calling. Uncle Henry and Dorothy follow her.)*
Aunt Em	Henry, Dorothy, come back. It's a cyclone coming! Quickly. Oh do hurry! *(She hurries into the house, opens the trap-door into the cellar and starts to go down.)*
Uncle Henry	*(Buffeting against the wind.)* Dorothy! Where are you? We must get to the cellar quickly. It's a whirlwind!
Dorothy	You go in. I can't find Toto. He's hiding from the thunder.
Uncle Henry	Don't worry about him. He'll look after himself. Hurry. *(He goes into the house and down the cellar.)*
Dorothy	Toto! Come on Toto. The thunder won't hurt you. I must find you! Oh, please come back. I can't go without you. *(The wind rises to a crescendo, spinning her like a top. There is a crash of thunder, and Dorothy can be heard calling Toto as she is carried further and further away. It is now pitch dark.)* *(A bird sings and when the Lights come back, the sky is blue and clear. Dorothy is lying on the ground where the wind dropped her. She slowly wakes up.)*
Dorothy	Uncle Henry, Aunt Em, where are you? *(Calling)* Where are you? *(She looks in her pocket and finds that Toto is there.)* Toto, there you are! Wherever are we? We must be a long way from home. I've never seen anywhere like this before. And I seem to have lost my shoes! *(The Good Witch of the North appears.)*
Good Witch	You are welcome, most noble Sorceress, to the land of the Munchkins.
Dorothy	*(Getting up and dusting herself.)* You are very kind.
Good Witch	We are grateful to you for having killed the Wicked Witch of the East and for setting our people free from her spell.
Dorothy	But I haven't killed anything.
Good witch	Well, your house did, and that is the same thing. See! The witch's shoes are still sticking out from underneath it.
Dorothy	*(Looking at them.)* Oh dear. I'm very sorry. The house was blown away by a strong wind, a cyclone my Uncle Henry called it. It must have fallen on her. What shall we do?

from *The Wizard of Oz,* a play by Alfred Bradley, from the novel
by L. Frank Baum (Samuel French Ltd.)

Author's notes

In adapting L. Frank Baum's classic children's novel for the theatre, I have simplified the plot and also enlarged the character of the Witch to balance the forces of good and evil. The original story is set in Kansas but this has been ignored as the characters don't belong to any particular country and for many actors an American accent is not easy.

This version of the play can be produced very simply, it needs no stage and may be performed in the round on the floor of a school hall. With a simplified setting, sound becomes very important: some of the effects like the whirlwind will need to be pre-recorded but a percussionist equipped with a wide range of accessories will emphasize the fun of the Scarecrow's falls, help the actors to move from one scene to another and generally add to the excitement.

🗝 Answer in sentences.

1 Uncle Henry is sharpening a scythe at the beginning of Act 1. What is a scythe used for? *(1 mark)*

2 In the novel, Toto is a little dog. Why do you think Alfred Bradley decided to change him into a mouse in the stage adaptation? *(1.5 marks)*

3 Aunt Em tells Dorothy that some storms have been so violent that ....
.... *(1 mark)*

4 The novel is set in Kansas. Why has Alfred Bradley deliberately made the characters from no "particular country"? *(1.5 marks)*

5 Dorothy is carried far away from her aunt and uncle by the cyclone. How is this suggested on stage? *(1.5 marks)*

6 What has happened to the Wicked Witch of the East? *(1 mark)*

7 Alfred Bradley says that his stage version can be produced very simply "in the round" in a school hall. What does "in the round" mean? *(1.5 marks)*

8 He says that sound effects will be very important. What sound effects are needed in this excerpt? *(1.5 marks)*

9 How does a clever use of lighting suggest that Dorothy and the house have been carried away by the cyclone? *(1.5 marks)*

10 List the "props" (objects and furniture used on stage) needed for this extract. *(1.5 marks)*

11 What sort of person is Dorothy? *(1.5 marks)*